OMAR KHAYYAM

This book explores the life and work of Omar Khayyam as a provocateur of peace. While Khayyam is known for his poetry, he was foremost a prominent mathematician who looked at the world from a unique perspective. Using the transformative power of mathematics, he brought together seemingly irreconcilable concepts in his work. Through his art, philosophy, and mathematics, Khayyam sought to create harmony between what on the surface looks like a clash between his scientific view, romantic and often provocative poetry, and philosophy. The book sheds light on his spiritual and philosophical journey through a cross-sectional account of his poetry, philosophical view, and mathematics and science. It explores the complex inner life of a multidimensional scholar as he negotiated between faith and science, constructing a framework for peace by looking at the world as it presents itself to us, contemplating the temporality of life and enriching it with wisdom and joy.

Historically and culturally informed, this book will be indispensable to readers of Omar Khayyam's poetry and philosophy. It will also be of interest to students and researchers of peace and conflict studies, mathematics, science, Middle East literature, history, and popular culture.

Nick M. Loghmani is the coauthor of *Harmony and Exchange: Toward a Legoic Society* (2017). A researcher and tech executive by day, author by night, he received his BSc in Mathematics from the University of Waterloo, Canada, and his MSc in Applied Data Science from Syracuse University, USA. He cofounded Solidarity with Iran, a diverse group that promotes inclusiveness and democratic principles, and is the coauthor of *Charter 91*, a blueprint for promoting new participatory avenues in Iran. He contributes to Radio Free Europe, BBC Persian, the Huffington Post, and Indian Seminar magazine. He divides his time between Toronto and San Francisco.

PEACEMAKERS
Series Editor: Ramin Jahanbegloo

Executive Director of the Mahatma Gandhi Centre for Nonviolence and Peace Studies and the Vice-Dean of the School of Law at Jindal Global University, India

Peace is one of the central concepts in the spiritual and political life of humanity. Peace does not imply the absence of war. It implies harmony, justice and empathy. Empathy is the key to education of peace in our world. In other words, despite the vast differences of values between cultures and traditions, it is still possible to grasp an understanding of one another, by "empathy". Throughout centuries, peacemakers have endorsed a "shared human horizon", which according to them had the critical force of avoiding moral anarchy and relativism while acknowledging the plurality of modes of being human.

Today in a different manner and in a changed tone, but with the same moral courage and dissenting voice, this series on "Peacemakers" offers the first comprehensive engagement with the problems of peace in our age, through a meticulous and thorough study of the lives and thoughts of peacemakers of all ages.

NELSON MANDELA
Peace Through Reconciliation
Neera Chandhoke

OMAR KHAYYAM
On the Value of Time
Nick M. Loghmani

For more information about this series, please visit: www.routledge.com/Peacemakers/book-series/PCMK

OMAR KHAYYAM

On the Value of Time

Nick M. Loghmani

LONDON AND NEW YORK

First published 2022
by Routledge
4 Park Square, Milton Park, Abingdon, Oxon OX14 4RN

and by Routledge
605 Third Avenue, New York, NY 10158

Routledge is an imprint of the Taylor & Francis Group, an informa business

© 2022 Nick M. Loghmani

The right of Nick M. Loghmani to be identified as author of this work has been asserted in accordance with sections 77 and 78 of the Copyright, Designs and Patents Act 1988.

All rights reserved. No part of this book may be reprinted or reproduced or utilised in any form or by any electronic, mechanical, or other means, now known or hereafter invented, including photocopying and recording, or in any information storage or retrieval system, without permission in writing from the publishers.

Trademark notice: Product or corporate names may be trademarks or registered trademarks, and are used only for identification and explanation without intent to infringe.

British Library Cataloguing-in-Publication Data
A catalogue record for this book is available from the British Library

Library of Congress Cataloging-in-Publication Data
A catalog record for this book has been requested

ISBN: 978-0-367-64075-0 (hbk)
ISBN: 978-1-032-00145-6 (pbk)
ISBN: 978-1-003-17293-2 (ebk)

DOI: 10.4324/9781003172932

Typeset in Sabon
by Apex CoVantage, LLC

To my parents, who encouraged my curiosity,
and to my friend and intellectual companion,
Ramin Jahanbegloo

CONTENTS

	Series Editor's Preface	viii
	Introduction	1
1	The World Khayyam Was Born Into	5
2	The Creative Space	14
3	Life as Integration of Moments	51
4	Khayyam, the Peace Provocateur	67
	Conclusion	100
	Appendix: A Stylometric Analysis of Khayyam's Poetry	110
	References	116
	Index	126

SERIES EDITOR'S PREFACE

Peace is one of the central concepts of the spiritual and political life of humanity. When we study the world's religious and philosophical teachings, whether they are from the East or the West, we see that one of the basic ideals of all religions is peace. Peace does not imply simply absence of war. It implies harmony, justice, and empathy. Empathy is the key to education of peace in our world. In other words, despite the vast differences of values between cultures and traditions, it is still possible to grasp an understanding of one another, by "empathy". Therefore, we can maintain that all cultures have a shared core of common humanity. Throughout centuries, peacemakers endorsed a "shared human horizon", which according to them had the critical force of avoiding moral anarchy and relativism while acknowledging the plurality of modes of being human. As a matter of fact, the first step for peacemakers has always been not only to assume that there are differences among nations, cultures, and traditions of thought but also to admit that people may have different value systems which need to be understood and approached dialogically and critically. Philosophy of peace is, thus, expressed here in the idea of a "self-respecting" community or nation which strives to remove its own imperfections instead of necessarily judging others. As a result, peacemaking is always a call not only to cultivate humility but also to foster pluralism. Such a view is essential if we are to avoid the danger of cultural conformity and move toward the recognition of shared values of humanity and the acceptance of what Martin Luther King, Jr. called the "cosmic companionship." Put it differently, we can say that it would be an error to hope that we can ever achieve a truly universal vision of peace without an intercultural approach to the idea of civilization. Peacemakers have always been in favor of a farsighted peacemaking in our world which has seriously advocated the logic of solidarity and civic friendship beyond national selfishness and global exclusion. Let us not forget that all peacemakers, either man or woman, young or old, from the West or the East, were all engaged in the process of peace seeking by fighting for care, openness, and empathy as constructive forms of being together. Today, in a different manner and in a changed tone, but with the same moral courage and dissenting voice, this series on "Peacemakers" offers the first comprehensive engagement with the problems of peace in our age, through a meticulous and thorough study of the lives and thoughts of peacemakers of all ages.

Ramin Jahanbegloo

INTRODUCTION

It is rare to come across a scholar that comprehends the world in a true multidimensional fashion and composes its complexity artistically and poetically. Without a doubt, Omar Khayyam was one of those, not only because of his talent, after all, few can match his claim to be a mathematician, philosopher, and poet, but because of the way he integrated his artistic view with his scientific and philosophical work.

Khayyam not only examined the challenging questions of his era but stood up against crushing forces that were working against freethinking and expanding the boundaries of knowledge and artistic expression.

Khayyam's unique way of life and worldview provides a glimpse into an intellectual mind ahead of his time. On the one hand, he engaged with the most challenging questions of being and existence. On the other hand, he used his artistic mind to challenge the same answer, thus shifting and displacing the borders of traditions and beliefs.

Khayyam's message is clear: our life is the integration of its moments. While we are gifted with time, it is up to us to make deliberate choices to turn it into meaningful moments, moments that emerge when coming in touch and interacting with art and elements of the world that can lead to creativity.

Khayyam's perspective on celebrating life and living it creatively reminds of Heidegger's concept of dwelling (Gordon, 2000):

INTRODUCTION

"Humans dwell on this earth Full of merit, but also poetically" (McWhorter and Stenstad, 2009).

Heidegger used the above lines from a poem by late Hölderlin to expand on the concept of dwelling and living life poetically; it helps us live authentically and truthfully and taking the measure of our existence.

Nine hundred years before Heidegger, Khayyam wrote:

> *Bulbuls, doting on roses, oft complain*
> *How forward breezes rend their veils in twain;*
> *Sit we beneath this rose, which many a time*
> *Has sunk to earth, and sprung from earth again.*
> (Khayyam and Whinfield, 1883, p. 67)

It is important to note that while the world knows Khayyam through his poetry, there is much more to his scholarly work and worldview that has been left unexamined thus far. It can be argued that Khayyam's poetry is just the tip of an iceberg of a scholar that used his wit and poetic aptitude in conjunction with his scientific prowess and philosophical insight to upend our understanding of the world and create an alternative approach to the question of life and afterlife. Therefore, to form an accurate picture of Khayyam and his worldview, one should consider the balance of his life. There is no doubt that Khayyam was a multidimensional intellectual and scholar. If approached from a single perspective, his work may contain seemingly contradictory positions. However, such controversies could be explained through a comprehensive examination of his philosophical, scientific, and artistic work.

There are few mathematicians in history known for their poetry—Khayyam is one of them—occupying a prominent position as a multidimensional figure: poet, philosopher, and mathematician.

While Khayyam is mostly known for his poetry, he was foremost a prominent mathematician. Khayyam looked at the world from a unique perspective, finding relations between seemingly irreconcilable concepts such as evil and existence

INTRODUCTION

and using the transformative power of mathematics to anchor mystical tradition to cosmological cycles' precision.

Khayyam lived in a tumultuous period when oppressive forces silenced any form of deviation from the preached religious tradition in the name of religion. In this hostile environment, Khayyam, through his art, philosophy, and math, created harmony between what on the surface looks like a clash between his scientific view, romantic and often provocative poetry, and deterministic philosophy.

This balancing act of creating a harmony between clashing ideas is the cornerstone of his work. While his poetry provokes the reader into forgoing abstinence, favoring worldly pleasures, his philosophy tries to delve into existence and essence. His work on devising a calendar tries to bring cosmological precision to divine cycles.

Khayyam's answer to crises of life and faith is a balancing act to maintain harmony between the seemingly opposing forces; as in this tension, he created creative space and peace. These pivotal times are part of Khayyam's spiritual and philosophical journey. He emerged from conflicts between faith and science intact, maintaining the balance, while others gave up on their faith or science.

Many books have delved into Khayyam's poetry, yet few have specifically addressed the cross section of his poetry, philosophical view, and mathematics. One of the most important titles, *Rubā'iyyāt*, offers an interpretation of Khayyam's poetry by Edward Fitzgerald. However, his work, which is often cited as loosely based on Khayyam's poetry, does not provide a complete picture of a complex and multidimensional intellectual.

While Khayyam's life is examined throughout the book, this is not a biography of Omar Khayyam. There are books that delve into aspects of his personal life using available resources. Still, the purpose of this book is to provide a balanced picture of Khayyam's work, according to his life, scientific, and artistic creation. The book's message is verified against historical and scientific evidence. Whenever a historical event's accuracy was in question, multiple sources have been used. Furthermore, the chapters include insights from a broad spectrum of scholarly sources.

It is worth mentioning that analyzing Khayyam's life is challenging. Yet, it is fascinating and rewarding because of his complex and multi-faceted work and worldview, which requires understanding his era's historical and political context and his time's intellectual and scientific condition. Khayyam created a perfect harmony between art, philosophy, and science while standing on the bridge between two critical periods of history.

1
THE WORLD KHAYYAM WAS BORN INTO

Abu'l Fath Omar ibn Ibrāhīm Khayyām, known as Omar Khayyām, was born in the early decades of the first millennium around 1048. The world at the beginning of the second millennium was going through a tectonic shift. The Western world was going through a struggle that would set the stage for the rise of significant powers and foundations of future nations in the centuries to come. Meanwhile, the Muslim world was going through its cultural zenith, with India and China experiencing the rise and expansion of new dynasties. The Byzantine empire experienced a sudden decline while Norman rose to power and domination over much of Europe. Catholicism asserted itself, and the split between Eastern Orthodoxy and Roman Catholicism became permanent (Cross and Livingstone, 2005).

The 11th century is considered the middle ages in Europe. In Western Europe, serfdom was imposed on a significant portion of the population. In England, the Viking age came to an end with King Canute and his son Harthacnut. In 1055, Westminster Abbey was completed, and in 1086, the doomsday book was compiled. In 1066 in the Battle of Hastings, Normans defeated the English Army. One of the notable developments in the 11th century was the foundation of the University of Oxford. It commenced its first lectures in 1096.

Like elsewhere, living a peaceful life was a challenge in most Europe—life was violent, short, and challenging. Religious skirmishes led to numerous wars and bloodshed that was the cause of significant harm and suffering for the peasantry. Following the collapse of the Carolingian Empire in the 9th century, the level of violence became so tense that it required intervention from the Catholic Church to limit violence perpetrated by the nobility (Ariès et al., 1987). It led to Truce of God, the first mass peace movement in history (Backman, 2009), at the Council of Toulouges in 1027.

In Spain, Muslims started to lose their grip. Alfonso VI of Castile defeated the Muslims and captured the city of Toledo in 1085, followed by El Cid conquering Valencia.

The Kingdom of France was emerging from Île-de-France, while Frankish Carolingian kings were struggling to keep order. Meanwhile, the aristocracy was transforming to retain and control political power.

In Bologna, currently, Italy, the University of Bologna, the oldest university in the world, was established (Janin, 2014).

The Song dynasty affirmed its power in China and established central authority by reducing regional commanders' ability. Confucian practice and influence grew, and the Chinese aristocracy transformed through a merit-based government system (Elman, 2013).

In 1008, Emperor Zhenzong of Song accepted the gifts from the Fatimid ruler of Egypt's Imam Al-Hakim bi-Amr Allah, reestablishing diplomatic relations between Egypt and China, lost since the collapse of the Tang dynasty (Shen, 1996).

In 1048, the movable type was invented by Bi Sheng in China (Needham and Ronan, 1978). In 1084, the historical work of the Zizhi Tongjian was compiled by Song dynasty scholars (Xiao-bin, 2003, pp. 1–32).

In India, Rajendra Chola I became the Chola empire king, succeeding his father, Rajaraja Chola. India was the target of numerous Ghaznavid campaigns during the 11th century (Saunders, 1947).

Japan was experiencing the Heian period, named after the capital city of Heian-kyō, modern-day Kyoto, with the imperial court and its associated aristocracy experiencing their zenith. Art and literature were at the focus of the court's aristocracy in this period (Britannica, 2013).

THE WORLD KHAYYAM WAS BORN INTO

During the Heian period, *The Tale of Genji*, often called the world's first novel, was written (Lyons, 2013).

In Germany, Henry II became the first to be called the "King of the German" (Whaley, 2018), the term Rex Teutonicorum (Eckhard, 1999, pp. 233–266), King of the Germans, came into use around 1000.

In 1099, Jerusalem was captured by the crusaders.

While the Muslim world was defending its western front, in the East, it was expanding in India and what is today Afghanistan.

The Muslim world rule was divided between the Seljuk dynasty and the Fatimid caliphate, following the decline of the Ghaznavid (Bosworth, 1975) dynasty, with Seljuk ruling over most Middle Eastern parts of Western Asia as well as Central Asia, including Persia, Anatolia. Fatimid (Brett, 2017) controlled Egypt, north African territories along the Mediterranean Sea, and Scilly and Levant.

Following the Arab conquest of Persia and the fall of the Sassanid empire, Persian identity and distinct cultural characteristics started to reemerge with poets and literary figures' work.

While the Arabic language hegemony dominated many local languages, particularly in Syria and Egypt, Persians resisted the dominance of Arab rulers. Still, they transformed it, as the Arab caliphs had to rely on Persian elites for their civilian administration (Morgan, 1976).

In 1010, Ferdowsi completed his epic work, the *Shahnameh*, arguably the most influential work in Persian literature history (Khaleghi-Motlagh, 2012).

Ibn Sina, or as known in the West, Avicenna, a figure that Khayyam considered himself as his student, passed away in 1037. Avicenna was arguably the most prominent and influential scientist and philosopher of the middle ages. He is regarded as the father of early modern medicine (Colgan, 2009).

While under house arrest in Egypt, Ibn al-Haytham produced his groundbreaking work, *Book of Optics* (Lindberg, 1976; Bīrūnī and Sachau, 1879).

Another towering figure of that time was Al Biruni, the anthropologist, mathematician, historian (Nasr, 1993),[1] and astronomer, who had an enormous contribution to the advancement and defense of science (George, 2021).

Al-Farabi passed away hundred years before Khayyam's birth. Still, he left his mark by contributing to the philosophy of society and religion (Germann, 2016), as well as in science, language (Druart, 2020), and music (Druart, 2020).

Asian countries dominated the world economy in the 11th century in technology, trade volumes, and GDP. Excluding Japan, Asian countries' GDP was almost eight times greater than Western Europe (Maddison, 2001).

West Asia, Persia in particular, played a pivotal role in trade between the West and the East, acting as a bridge for commerce and technology and, equally importantly, culture and philosophy. The merchants did not only import silk and spices from the far East but brought books and ideas. While Europe had, for the most part, Europe had forgotten the Greek philosophers and their work (Dod, 1982). They were translated and widely used by philosophers of the Islamic era in Baghdad, Nishabur, and Damascus. Philosophical work of the Islamic world eventually found its way through Sicily and Spain to Europe, which helped revive philosophy in the West. This revival led to Thomas Aquinas's work to establish a relationship between faith and reason in his work Summa Theologica (Flannery, 2001) (1265–1274), based on reconciling the teaching of Aristotle with Christianity.

Omar Khayyam was born (Ross and Gibb, 1929) in 1048[2] in Nishapur (Honigmann and Bosworth) (today Nishabur) Khorasan, Persia, modern-day Iran. At the time of Khayyam's birth, Nishabur was one of the most prominent cities of the medieval time—a cultural and trade center situated on the Silk Road, connecting the East and the West. It was a familiar city for merchants traveling through the Silk Road, which was considered a passage for not only goods but ideas and adventurous souls curious about the four corners of the world (Frankopan, 2015).

The city of Nishabur, meaning New-Shahpur in middle Farsi, was founded by the Sasanid king Shahpur I in the 3rd century. Nishabur had a tumultuous history. By the 11th century, it had already witnessed numerous wars, devastating earthquakes, and the ruin of various dynasties. While its walls carried the scars of history, its rich soil ensured its lavish gardens' rejuvenation. After each disaster, Nishabur rose again like a phoenix from its ashes.

At the time of Khayyam's birth, Nishabur was at the height of its prosperity. It was famous for its poetry (Encyclopedia Britannica, 2018), turquoise mines, and being a hub of art and culture.

Khayyam's parents paid attention to his education. His father, Ebrahim, was apparently converted from Zoroastrianism to Islam (Aminrazavi, 2007). Khayyam's family was wealthy as his father worked as a physician to ensure that his son received good schooling. He hired mathematician Bahmanyar bin Marzban, a Zoroastrian mathematician and student of Avicenna, as a young Khayyam tutor.

Bahmanyar was no ordinary tutor, his interaction with Avicenna resulted in several works, notably *al-Mubāḥathāt* ("The Discussions") and *Kitāb al-taḥṣīl* ("The Summation"), which was a summary of Avicenna works (Garakani and Brown, 2013) on logic, physics, and metaphysics.

Bahmanyar's in-depth knowledge of Avicenna's work influenced young Khayyam as he received a thorough education in mathematics, philosophy, and science.

Khayyam himself was a devotee of Avicenna and wrote a treatise on Avicenna's work and referenced him in *On Being and Necessity*:

> What remains from among the most important and difficult problems [to solve] is the difference among the order of existents. . . . Perhaps I, and my teacher, the master of all who has proceeded before him, Avicenna, have thoughtfully reflected upon this problem, and to the extent that it is satisfactory to our intellects, we have understood it.
> (Aminrazavi and Brummelen, 2017)

Khayyam lost his father Ebrahim and his tutor Bahmanyar a few months apart as he was turning 18, which coincided with

Halley's Comet appearance, giving the future astronomer a chance to observe unique astronomical objects.

While the introduction and spread of paper and paper making (Floor, 2005) techniques facilitated the exchange and spread of ideas, it was not easy to be a free thinker in the 11th century. The golden era of philosophy in the Islamic world was starting to come to a close. The world that Khayyam was born in was not kind to free philosophers and intellectuals. His much-admired predecessor Avicenna spent time in jail for corresponding to leave his position as a vizier and move to a different city (Gutas, 2011). Opposition to established religious orthodoxy and sometimes suspicion of it was enough to jeopardize a scholar's life. Abu Hamid al-Ghazali's opposition to philosophy and science is often cited as contributing to the decline of philosophy and science in the Islamic world. However, some argue that he was the symptom rather than the cause for shuttering the space of debate and freethinking (Farabi et al., 2001). Al-Farabi's thesis saw religion as a vessel for humans to achieve perfection and happiness in the world while al-Ghazali occasionalism injected God's intervention in every aspect of life. Shifting from Al-Farabi's rationalist approach to Al-Ghazali occasionalism meant negating the use of logic and rationality in the world and effectively supplanting logic with faith.

Ghazali's worldview was adopted and spread by Nezamiye's school, devised and financed by the powerful grand vizier of the Seljuks dynasty, Nizam al-Mulk (Mansouri, 2013).

> Al-Ghazali had studied under the formidable al-Juwayni (1028–1085), who had helped Nizam al-Mulk to formulate his religious policy. It may have been al-Juwayni's experience of contemporary politics that led him to the view, remarkably for a religious Jurist, that "the imam was first and foremost a political and military leader whose descent had no bearing on his competence".
>
> (Black, 2011)

Nezamiye's rule in spreading and reinforcing religious studies at the expense of independent inquiry led to purging scientific investigations.

Nezamiye schools institutionalized religious study and became a de facto political tool to produce one-dimensional scholars trained not to think outside the dogmatic religious orthodoxy rail guards.

Khayyam grew up in a world where intellectual life was increasingly under attack by Sharia orthodoxy, on the one hand, and by mystical concerns, on the other.

According to some accounts, Khayyam was reserved and inconspicuous, and humble. Khayyam's lack of interest in accepting students should be considered in the context of a hostile environment toward free thinkers and the kind of rebellious view that he was advocating in Rubaiyat.

> *The secrets which my book of love has bred,*
> *Cannot be told for fear of loss of head;*
> *Since none is fit to learn, or cares to know,*
> *'Tis better all my thoughts remain unsaid.*
> (Tirtha and Khayyam, 1941, p. 266)

In or around the year 1068, aged 20, Khayyam left Nishabur for Samarkand, a center of scholarship at the time, where he composed his famous treatise on algebra.

In the following years (around 1973), Khayyam was appointed to revise the Persian calendar. Subsequently, he led a group of scientists and set up an observatory in Isfahan, where Khayyam and his team are said to have carried the most precise calculation of the length of the year (Bolt et al., 2007) at the time. The result of their work was the Jalali Calendar, named in honor of Malik Shah (Malcolm, 2011). Jalali Calendar was the most precise calendar of its era and more accurate than the Gregorian Calendar of 1582 (Frye, 1975).

Following Malik Shah's death, Khayyam took to Mecca for pilgrimage, allegedly to put at rest the suspicion of skepticism and deviance from the established orthodox reading of Islam.

Following his retirement from Sultan Sanjar's court, he returned to Nishabur to continue his intellectual journey in seclusion.

Khayyam lived in an era where religion was becoming an instrument of power, which, to gain efficiency, required enforcing hegemony and suppressing pluralism. The instrumentalization of religion had a disastrous impact on creativity and freedom of thought. In the Islamic world, the consequence was dire, effectively ending the golden era of scientific discovery and philosophical inquiry.

Khayyam's life was a struggle to keep his freedom of thought in an environment that refusing the established orthodoxy was becoming increasingly difficult and at times even dangerous, to the extent that being a philosopher was an act of heresy.

> *My enemies call me a philosopher,*
> *But God knows full well they greatly err;*
> *I know not even what I am, much less*
> *Why on this earth I am a sojourner.*
>
> (Khayyam and Whinfield, 1980a)

Khayyam found liberation in art, using his poetry to expand his creative space and challenge and ridicule the established orthodoxy, even at times questioning his faith and philosophical positions.

> *Of mosque and prayer and fast preach not to me,*
> *Rather go drink, were it on charity!*
> *Yea, drink, Khayyam, your dust will soon be made*
> *A jug, or pitcher, or a cup, may be!*
>
> (Khayyam et al., 1903, p. 244)

Like an equilibrist, Khayyam walked the tightrope of freethinking, using art and science to maintain his balance and push the boundary of knowledge forward. As Albert Camus said (Jahanbegloo, 2020), "To create today is to create dangerously.

Any publication is an act, and that act exposes one to the passions of an age that forgives nothing."

Notes

1 Al Birouni completed *The Remaining Signs of Past Centuries*, a book on the significance of calendars in different cultures and civilizations, rich with mathematical, astronomical, and historical information.
2 An account if his horoscope by the historian Beyhaqi is used by modern scholars to establish his birth on May 18, 1048. "he was Gemini, the sun and Mercury being in the ascendant."

2
THE CREATIVE SPACE

Being a free thinker among followers is never easy, particularly in a world of dogmatic rulers and jurists who see it upon themselves to shepherd the masses toward heaven, be it by burning those disobedient souls in the fire of earthly hell. While Khayyam, like his predecessor scholar Razi (Strousma, 1999), accepted the principle of God as the creator, he did not adhere to the dogmatic reading of the religion. To understand Khayyam and his intellectual worldview, one should consider his philosophical position in light of his artistic work. For instance, while analyzing being and existence in his philosophy, he questions the same standing in his poetry, sometimes mocking the certitude of—know it all—sages and jurists.

> *Some for the Glories of this World; and some*
> *Sigh for the Prophet's Paradise to come;*
> *Ah, take the Cash, and let the Credit go,*
> *Nor heed the rumble of a distant Drum!*
> (FitzGerald, 1997)

It is essential to expand on the notion of creativity and how Khayyam used it to expand the realm of possibilities and challenge the established beliefs and norms, including his philosophical standing.

Creativity is fundamental to the progress of humanity, from art to science and technology. It can be argued that creativity is what sets us apart from other biological forms. Creativity enables us to transcend our physical limitations and create an imaginary world, unconstrained by the physical World's rules and regulations. In summary, we are the only creature on the earth with a mind that can imagine the impossible.

Creativity is an expansion of space of possibilities, removing the boundaries of interaction between individuals and their ideas. In other words, creativity is not limited to creating objects or art forms but as a way of being and human experience.

As John Dewey (1934) explained in his book *Art as Experience*, art emerges from the artist's interaction with the world. It is the human experience that brings art and action together.

As Dewey puts it, art:

> is a developing process. . . . the artist finds where he is going because of what he has previously done; that is, the original excitation and stir of some contact with the World undergo successive transformation. The state of the matter he has arrived at sets up demands to be fulfilled, and it institutes a framework that limits further operations.
>
> (p. 116)

Therefore, art emerges from the artist's creative interaction with the world. The creative expression stands at the intersection of the artist and the art object (Benson, 1993).

Khayyam's appreciation of the moment, spent on interaction with the beauty, should be analyzed from this perspective. In Khayyam's worldview, life is a potential for creativity, where the art of living is the act of being with beauty and expanding the creative space.

> *And if the Wine you drink, the Lip you press,*
> *End in the Nothing all Things end in-Yes-*
> *Then fancy while Thou art, Thou art but what*
> *Thou shalt be-Nothing-Thou shalt not be less.*
>
> (Khayyam et al., 1997)

Expanding the creative space is an act of liberation, as it requires moving the boundaries of beliefs and what limits the individual creative force.

The act of throwing off the psychological yoke, imposed by tradition and demand of obedience, liberates the senses and thoughts to see and experience the new space, where imagination can be unleashed to create a new form of interaction.

Khayyam's insistence on being present to the moment should be considered from this perspective, as happiness without creativity would lead to everydayness and dullness.

> *Since naught we hold in hand of ought but air,*
> *Since ought in hand is but of vain affair,*
> *Presume it aught: what thou perceive is not!*
> *Assume it naught: what thou conceive is there!*
>
> (Parchizadeh, 2010)

Happiness and joy emerge from the act of discovery; it can be said that sustaining happiness depends on creative interaction with the world. Therefore, happiness cannot be ritualistic, as repetitive interaction with the world would not expand the creative space and discover new possibilities.

It is essential to note the difference between the contemplative practice of discovery and mindless receptive rituals. While the former is active and expands the boundaries of possibilities, the latter is passive, formalized, and limited to the criteria set by the social or religious practices.

It is worth mentioning Maurice Bloch's influential theory of ritual. According to Maurice Bloch, as ritual dictates not only the manner and style of utterance but its vocabulary and syntax, it induces "acceptance, compliance, or at least forbearance with regard to any overt challenge." Bloch argues that limiting what can be said and how it is expressed prohibits the act of rebellion, leaving revolution as the only feasible alternative. According to Bloch, rituals support traditional forms of social hierarchy and authority, promoting the social status quo. Therefore, the political and artistic challenge of the status quo requires questioning of rituals (Bell, 1997).

What necessitates rebellion is the immutability and inflexibility of rituals that put it in contrast with creativity. Happiness emerges from interaction with the world that is creative and inventive rather than ritualistic. To better understand the role of rituals in preventing social change, it is necessary to refer to Catherine Bell's notable work on rituals. According to Bell (1992), ritualization is "a way of acting that is designed and orchestrated to distinguish and privilege what is being done in comparison to other, usually more quotidian, activities." It is the conservation and privilege of rituals that stand in the way of change and transformation (Bell, 1992, p. 74).

The relationship between ritualization and institutionalization is essential, as institutionalization transforms the social space by enforcing specific modes of interaction and governance. Through the institutionalization of the rituals, the establishment gains the legitimacy and ability to control social space.

According to Alec Stone Sweet and et al.,

> Social spaces are arenas, or recurrent situations, wherein actors orient their actions to one another repeatedly. We call a social space "institutionalized" when there exists a widely shared system of rules and procedures to define who actors are, how they make sense of each other's actions, and what types of action are possible. Institutionalization is the process by which a social space emerges and evolved.
> (Sweet et al., 2001)

The emerging social space is guarded by the establishment as it is employed to preserve the power structure and mode of interactions that yield the best social and economic value for it.

What stands in the way of creativity is not the rituals or the emerging social space but the lethargy and immutability of the institutions guarding them. In other words, creativity and ritualization are not inherently at odds; it is the resistance of the emerged "social space" to the transformative power of creativity that inhibits change and curb creative space.

In his Rubaiyat, Khayyam invites us to question the wisdom of the most fundamental aspects of our belief system, death, and the afterlife.

> *"How sweet is mortal Sovranty!"—think some:*
> *Others—"How blest the Paradise to come!"*
> *Ah, take the Cash in hand and waive the Rest;*
> *Oh, the brave Music of a distant Drum!"*
>
> (Khayyam and FitzGerald, 1997)

The question is what motivates Khayyam to oppose the common belief about the afterlife; after all, in his philosophical work, he does not refute the notion of life after death (Aminrazavi and Brummelen, 2017). One should look for the answer in Khayyam's view about the value of time. The concept of the eternal afterlife, with its atemporality, contradicts the scarce time of earthly life; furthermore, the key to entering the timeless afterlife is through repetitive and immutable rituals, far from the creative and exciting life Khayyam is advocating.

The immutability of the afterlife is in contrast with the possibility of creativity. What is immutable has no past and no future; its timelessness makes the concert of moments meaningless as it cannot be pregnant with change. Khayyam's worldview is in clear contrast with an unchangeable afterlife. As for a creative poet and free thinker, what is more frightening than being condemned to a life devoid of art and possibilities? In other words, what makes this world interesting is its potency for change and openness to creative destruction. Khayyam's view on death is not a means to reach salvation but as a boundary and limit for the moments of our life. Death is the destruction of what is old; it clears the path for new possibilities and transformation. In that sense, death and creativity share the same characteristic; destruction as a mode of creation.

As John Fisher puts it:

> Destruction has always meant the change of an organized object into a relatively disorganized one, or the annihilation of the features which made it what it

once was. Artistic creation has always meant a new order, the bringing into being of something new, or the translation of knowledge or idea into a new form, with form, always indicating a spatial object.

(Fisher, 1974)

Death transforms the human body into dust, which turns into clay and may be used by a potter to create a jug of wine.

"Of mosque and prayer and fast preach not to me,
Rather go drink, were it on charity!
Yea, drink, Khayyam, your dust will soon be made
A jug, or pitcher, or a cup, may be!"

(Khayyam et al., 1903)

It is the destructive power of death that gives meaning to the moments of life, and it is the scarcity of time that makes its moments precious.

From doubt to clear assurance is a breath,
A breath from infidelity to faith;
O precious breath! enjoy it while you may,
'Tis all that life can give, and then comes death.

(Khayyam and Whinfield, 2013, p. 18)

The concept of eternal life is an attempt to make death less salient and influential on the life in this world, attributing timelessness to the afterlife as a trade-off of temporal worldly life is an economic activity; it compels humans to trade their time in this world with the promise of eternal life in heaven, condemning those who refuse to never-ending punishment in hell.

Oh, threats of Hell and Hopes of Paradise!
One thing at least is certain—This Life flies;
One thing is certain and the rest is Lies;
The Flower that once has blown for ever dies.

(Khayyam and FitzGerald, 1997)

Khayyam challenges the idea of giving up the present in favor of an unknown and unverifiable afterlife. He ridicules the trade as selling the life short for a questionable credit.

> *"How sweet is mortal Sovranty!"—think some:*
> *Others—"How blest the Paradise to come!"*
> *Ah, take the Cash in hand and waive the Rest;*
> *Oh, the brave Music of a distant Drum!*
>
> (Khayyam and FitzGerald, 1997)

Khayyam seeks happiness in the present and real life. He invites us to create joyous moments in this life rather than resigning to passivity. While the latter dictates obedience, the former is an act of rebellion and requires creativity. Khayyam takes the concept of death and turns it into a creative force, a transformative stage in the world.

> *All forms that perish other forms supply,*
> *(By turns we catch the vital breath and die)*
> *Like bubbles on the sea of matter borne,*
> *They rise, they break, and to that sea return.*
>
> (Pope, 1733)

> *Let us shake off dull reason's incubus,*
> *Our tale of days or years cease to discuss,*
> *And take our jugs, and plenish them with wine,*
> *Or e'er grim potters make their jugs of us!*
>
> (Khayyam et al., 1940)

The transformative power of death arises from its definiteness and certainty, as every living being is destined to die. By placing a limit on the temporal dimension of life, death transforms the value of its moments. Life is bounded between birth, creation, death, and destruction. The cycle of creation-destruction is how the world renews itself. In other words, death is a necessary stage of the creative process.

> *Bulbuls, doting on roses, oft complain*
> *How froward breezes rend their veils in twain;*
> *Sit we beneath this rose, which many a time*
> *Has sunk to earth, and sprung from earth again.*
> (Khayyam et al., 1940)

While the state of consciousness after death has been the subject of debate for centuries, what is known for sure is that there is no access to the consciousness of dead people.

> *Go to! Cast dust on those deaf skies, who spurn*
> *Thy orisons and bootless prayers, and learn*
> *To quaff the cup, and hover round the fair;*
> *Of all who go, did ever one return?*
> (Khayyam et al., 1940)

> *We buy new wine and old, our cups to fill,*
> *And sell for two grains this World's good and ill;*
> *Know you where you will go to after death?*
> *Set wine before me, and go where you will!*
> (Khayyam et al., 1940)

The termination of consciousness means the end of personal experience in the world and the ability to assert one's will. Death puts an end to choice and power of will, even if one believes in the idea of the afterlife. If free will exists in the afterlife, then a person in heaven can make choices that, according to religious standard, could be considered sinful.

As Kevin Timpe (2013) says,

> if the redeemed are kept from sinning, their wills must be reined in, at least in some way. And if their wills are reined in, it doesn't seem right to say that they are free.

Therefore, it can be argued that there is less choice in heaven compared to life on the earth. Furthermore, a creative space that has the possibility of sinful choices would follow the same logic and thus would be forbidden (Martin, 1997).

There is an obvious trade-off here, assured temporal life on the earth with unlimited choice and possibilities versus an unverifiable afterlife with limited choice but infinite time.

Khayyam points out that since the afterlife is unverifiable, making such trade-offs is meaningless.

> *To-day is but a breathing space, quaff wine!*
> *Thou wilt not see again this life of thine;*
> *So, as the World becomes the spoil of time,*
> *Offer thyself to be the spoil of wine!*
> (Khayyam and Whinfield, 1980a, p. 20)

> *Drunkards are doomed to hell, so men declare,*
> *Believe it not, 'tis but a foolish scare;*
> *Heaven will be empty as this hand of mine,*
> *If none who love good drink find entrance there.*
> (Khayyam and Whinfield, 1980a, p. 67)

Khayyam's insistence on appreciating the moments of earthly life is not aroused by his hedonistic desires but his drive for creativity and learning about the secret of this world. Pleasure derived from sensation is limited in duration and is subject to loss of sensitivity and becoming habitual. On the other hand, creativity is not subject to the same limitation and can be the source of infinite possibilities. While the former provides limited choice, the latter offers unbounded possibilities.

Khayyam's poetry is a sign of courage not only in the face of tyranny and dogmatism but challenging his philosophical positions. Khayyam does not seek pleasure from a bottle of wine or philandering, as the pleasure derived from them wanes with their frequency, neither is his reference to earthly delights a metaphor for worshiping a metaphysical god. Khayyam references wine literals to enrich the moment of life and enjoy it; however, it must be noted that it is the subject of enrichment and moments of life that is paramount to him.

Khayyam's view on living a life of nobility, seeking knowledge and excellence, is arguably Aristotelian. Khayyam's worldview advocates happiness through choice, to choose the earthly life over promises of the afterlife. In other words, he invites us to have the courage to exist.

> *Since naught we hold in hand of ought but air,*
> *Since ought in hand is but of vain affair,*
> *Presume it aught: what thou perceive is not!*
> *Assume it naught: what thou conceive is there!*
> (Parchizadeh, 2010)

Khayyam's genius is his ability to create a harmony between his scientific and philosophical work and his poetry. For instance, since the moon was once a romantic subject of many poems, it can be argued that modern science has eroded its sentimental potency. Since humans stepped on the surface of the moon, its position radically shifted in our psyche, transformed it into a subject of science that needs to be examined and therefore dominated.

Khayyam has successfully created the harmony between science, philosophy, and art; while methodically observing moon cycles and their relation to the earth with mathematical precision, he masterfully revealed the romantic aspect in his poetry:

> *Since no one can assure thee of the morrow,*
> *Rejoice thy heart to-day, and banish sorrow*
> *With moon bright wine, fair moon, for heaven's moon*
> *Will look for us in vain on many a morrow.*
> (Khayyam and Whinfield, 1980a, p. 62)

Preserving the balance between rationality and romanticism is evident in many of Khayyam's work; his meticulous approach in his scientific and philosophical work is a hallmark of a rationalist scholar, while his poetry reveals a rebellious artist that sees the world as a blank canvas and his poetry as a means of creation.

Khayyam saw life as connected moments, like beads of a rosary. However, unlike a prayer rosary, Khayyam's moments are spent appreciating the beauty and apprehension of the world's mysteries.

> *From doubt to clear assurance is a breath,*
> *A breath from infidelity to faith;*
> *Oh, precious breath I enjoy it while you may,*
> *'Tis all that life can give, and then comes death.*
> (Khayyam and Whinfield, 1980b, p. 74)

Khayyam invites us to live a creative life, seize the moment, and see the world as it presents itself.

As an astronomer, Khayyam knew cosmological cycles quite well. After all, he observed and predicted their movement with astonishing accuracy to create the most precise calendar of his time. Khayyam's observation of celestial bodies movement was a matter of science which can be calculated with precision, enabling him to predict when the full moon will be illuminating Naishapur for the next thousand years, while no one can foresee the future of the city and its inhabitants, the moon would be predictable, following the same orbit around the earth.

While Khayyam saw cosmology as predictable and deterministic, his poetry points to his belief in free will and the concept of choice. Khayyamian time is discrete moments that emerge when one interacts with what fuels imagination and kindles creativity and appreciation of beauty.

In other words, meaningful moments are the result of interaction with the aesthetic aspect of the world. Listening to a masterpiece by Mozart is summoning the art to revitalize and inspire the moment. As a work of a genius mind, like Midas's touch, art transforms the moment of its audience, expanding the boundaries of possibilities, inspiring them, and filling their moment with appreciation and joy (Clark, 1973).

The delight of creativity is the antidote to the anxiety of the temporality of our existence. Khayyam's poetry addresses the complex relationship between the seeming meaninglessness of our existence and the beauty and mystery of this world. He points to joyous moments of life and their importance while reminding the temporal aspect of our existence. On the one hand, he warns against attaching meaning to life after death, while on the other, he is asking to enrich the moment of life through interacting with its beauty and wonders.

There is joy in interaction with what is beautiful, in both the objective, as something that exists in its own right and subjective form, as experienced through a mental process. For example, listening to a masterfully played symphony is interaction with beauty—the person is the subject that experiences the interaction with the object, the artistically composed music. It can be argued that interaction creates the experience. The exchange, if done consciously, creates the aesthetic experience that gives meaning to the moment.

> *And if the Wine you drink, the Lip you press,*
> *End in the Nothing all Things end in-Yes-*
> *Then fancy while Thou art, Thou art but what*
> *Thou shalt be-Nothing-Thou shalt not be less.*
> (Khayyam et al., 1997)

Aesthetic experience is central to Khayyam's poetry. He portrays life as temporary—we do not know its beginning and cannot comprehend its ending, with death being the only sure thing. He ridicules the idea of the afterlife and cast doubts about its existence. In other words, he strips our lives of all metaphysical and mystical layers that clutter our judgment and prevent us from seeing and grasping the world as it presents itself to us.

> *Oh, threats of Hell and Hopes of Paradise!*
> *One thing at least is certain—This Life flies;*
> *One thing is certain and the rest is Lies;*
> *The Flower that once has blown for ever dies.*
> (Khayyam and FitzGerald, 1910)

Khayyam's message is clear—existence is transient, and therefore exquisite moments of life should be valued. It means that in light of scarce time, it is imperative to cultivate a sense of presence and appreciation for beauty.

> *Who e'er returned of all that went before,*
> *To tell of that long road they travel o'er?*
> *Leave naught undone of what you have to do,*
> *For when you go, you will return no more.*
> (Khayyam and Whinfield, 1980a, p. 141)

Philosophy is the result of searching for truth, questioning, and finding answers about life and its mysteries. Aesthetics is also the result of that same need. Without aesthetics, life is incomplete, as it would lack a sense of meaning and direction. Khayyam's philosophical work and his poetry should be viewed in the same context as an intellectual and artistic pursuit of meaning in life.

> *life passes by, like a hurried caravan, Seize those joyous moments, Oh Saghi, let go of tomorrow's worries, set fort the chalice, for the night is on the march.*[1]

The temporary nature of life makes its moments precious, moments that become meaningful through the aesthetic experience of interacting with art and beauty. Therefore it can be argued that making moments is an aesthetic expression of time.

> *Yield not to grief, though fortune prove unkind,*
> *Nor call sad thoughts of parted friends to mind;*
> *Devote thy heart to sugary lips, and wine,*
> *Cast not thy precious life unto the wind!*
> (Khayyam and Fitzgerald, 1910)

It is important to note that when Khayyam was writing the *Rubaiyat*, Sufism and religious orthodoxy both were promoting anti-aesthetic asceticism, which forbade sensual pleasure, arguing that interacting with beauty would prevent one from pursuing spiritual goals.

While Islam strongly advocated asceticism, Zoroastrianism forbade fasting and mortification and promoted a life based on good words, good thought, and good deeds (Britannica, 2013). While Khayyam was not a Zoroastrian, one of his teachers was the mathematician Bahmanyar (d. 1067 CE), a former student of the great scholar and physician Avicenna (l. 980–1037 CE). Bahmanyar was a former Zoroastrian who had converted to Islam, and he might have taught Zoroastrian/Zorvanist concepts to young Khayyam.

> *Of mosque and prayer and fast preach not to me,*
> *Rather go drink, were it on charity!*
> *Yea, drink, Khayyam, your dust will soon be made*
> *A jug, or pitcher, or a cup, may be!*
>
> (Khayyam and Fitzgerald, 1910, p. 414)

While the influence of Zoroastrianism on Khayyam is open for debate, his writings and Zoroastrianism teaching have elements with similar traits, in particular, Zoroastrianism's emphasis on bringing happiness into this world through good deeds, good thoughts, and good words, which are deemed essential in the fight against evil. Khayyam's poetry also emphasizes avoiding evil and interacting with what is beautiful and just.

> *Ah, my Belovéd, fill the Cup that clears*
> *Today of past Regrets and future Fears:*
> *Tomorrow!—Why, Tomorrow I may be*
> *Myself with Yesterday's Sev'n thousand Years.*
>
> (Khayyam and Fitzgerald, 1910, p. 414)

While Khayyam's freedom from orthodoxies and traditions is best reflected in his poetry, his scientific work also clearly demonstrates a daring scientist not afraid to challenge his time's well-established beliefs and theories.

In his struggle, he had to face and endure the hostility of established orthodoxy and the disdain of mystic masters of his era, particularly Abu Hammid Ghazali, who, among other mystics, "viewed Khayyam not as a fellow-mystic, but a free-thinking scientist" (Frye, 1975).

> *My enemies call me a philosopher,*
> *But God knows full well they greatly err;*
> *I know not even what I am, much less*
> *Why on this earth I am a sojourner.*
>
> (Whinfield, 1893)

As demonstrated in many of his poems, his freethinking approach to essential questions of life challenged the belief system promoted by the religious jurists and mystic masters. The pursuit of aesthetics and avoiding asceticism is a crucial aspect of Khayyam's worldview. It can be argued that such a worldview is emancipating, as it is an invitation to free oneself from the shackles of dogma and traditions and be open to the beauty and wonder of the world.

> *Of mosque and prayer and fast preach not to me,*
> *Rather go drink, were it on charity!*
> *Yea, drink, Khayyam, your dust will soon be made*
> *A jug, or pitcher, or a cup, may be!*
>
> (Heron-Allen et al., 1908, p. 244)

Khayyam saw little value in spending time pursuing unprovable promises of the afterlife along with its rewards and punishments. What good, abstaining from beauty and joy and imposing abstinence and suffering, would do for the almighty creator of the universe. Khayyam complains about our pain and meaninglessness of suffering in this world; he expresses his disbelief in religious advocacy for reaching the truth through self-imposed hardship and avoiding the pleasant aspect of life, framing them as earthly and an obstacle in the path to heaven.

THE CREATIVE SPACE

It can be argued that Khayyam sees heaven and hell on the earth, the latter as endless suffering, pain, and violence, and the former as what brings us pleasure and joy. One is meaningless, oppressive, and monotonous, while the other is creative, diverse, and complex.

> *Nor quite a Giaour; my faith, indeed,*
> *May startle some who hear me say,*
> *I'd give my pilgrim staff away,*
> *And sell my turban, for an hour*
> *Of music in a fair one's bower.*
> *I'd sell the rosary for wine.*
> *Though holy names around it twine.*
> *And prayers the pious make so long,*
> *Are turned by me to joyous song;*
> *Or, if a prayer I should repeat.*
> *It is at my beloved's feet.*
>
> (Horne, 1917, pp. 13–14)

Suffering can be toxic to creativity and drain moments of their meaning. Since the value of time is paramount in Khayyam's poetry, he sees no point in toil and pain. Religious orthodoxy and mystic passivity are the jaws of oppressive practices that reduce life to repetitive cycles in pursuit of an imaginary mirage, ambiguous and inaccessible to humans' intellect.

> *Bygone days, do not mourn*
> *For tomorrow, do not yearn*
> *Settle not, on past or what's to come*
> *Rejoice now, do not throw life to the wind.*[2]

As a fundamental dimension of creativity, focusing on time is essential for freedom from repetition and suffering. Khayyam's attention to the value of time is not to fulfill hedonistic desires but to set free from limited immutable concepts and rituals that reduce the world into a closed space of interaction. Among contemporary philosophers, Henri Bergson's theory of time is notable. Bergson defines duration, as the interior temporal dimension, to be the dimension of freedom,

> While the external object does not bear the mark of the time that has elapsed and thus, in spite of the difference of time, the physicist can again encounter identical elementary conditions, duration is something real for the consciousness which preserves the trace of it, and we cannot here speak of identical conditions, because the same moment does not occur twice.
>
> It is no use arguing that, even if there are no two deep-seated psychic states which are altogether alike, yet analysis would resolve these different states into more general and homogeneous elements which might be compared with each other. This would be to forget that even the simplest psychic elements possess a personality and a life of their own, however superficial they may be; they are in a constant state of becoming, and the same feeling, by the mere fact of being repeated, is a new feeling. Indeed, we have no reason for calling it by its former name save that it corresponds to the same external cause or projects itself outwardly into similar attitudes: hence it would simply be begging the question to deduce from the so-called likeness of two conscious states that the same cause produces the same effect. In short, if the causal relation still holds good in the realm of inner states, it cannot resemble in any way what we call causality in nature.
>
> (Bergson, 2016, pp. 199–201)

While hundreds of years apart, there is a similar theme in Bergson's theory and Khayyam's poetry, Bergson's interpretation of time as a dimension of creativity with many multiplicities. Khayyam saw time as an opportunity to interact with the aesthetic aspect of life which is not far from Bergson's take on time. Time is a dimension of creativity, an opportunity to experience freedom.

Khayyam's time emerges from interaction with aesthetic elements of life. Being with what is beautiful is an experience that cannot be seized, replicated, or molded into a pattern to be reproduced. It is an individual experience that requires being attentive and present to space-time. Furthermore, it requires making choices to be in the same space-time of beauty, as embodied by a person, work of art, or nature.

> *O friend! let us not worry about tomorrow*
> *seize the brief life*
> *tomorrow we depart this transient world*
> *to company those went seven thousand years.*[3]

Khayyam questions the rationality of evil in the world, as it cannot be rationally reconciled with an omnipotent, omnibenevolent, and omniscient God. He laments the lack of will for birth and death and agonizes about the evil and suffering in the world. So if evil cannot be attributed to the creator, what can justify all the suffering and violence in the world? After all, we are thrown into this world and depart from it without a choice. Is there a connection between the existence of evil and our birth and death?

Qāḍī Abū Naṣr inquired Khayyam about the problem of evil:

> It is therefore necessary that the Necessary Being be the cause of the emergence of evil, opposition and corruption in the World. This is not worthy of Divine status. So how can we resolve this problem and the conflict so evil will not be attributed to the Necessary Being?
> (Ḍarurat al-taḍād fi'l-'ālam wa'l-jabr wa'l-baqā', Malik)
> (Aminrazavi and Brummelen, 2017)

While in his philosophical work Khayyam attributes evil to nothingness, in his poetry, he seems to be blaming God for our suffering and toil.

> *The Master did himself these vessels frame,*
> *Why should he cast them out to scorn and shame?*

If he has made them well, why should he break them?
Yea, though he marred them, they are not to blame.
(Khayyam and Whinfield, 1980b, p. 86)

However, in another quadrant, he recognizes the humans as the source of good and evil

The good and evil with man's nature blent,
The weal and woe that heaven's decrees have sent,
Impute them not to motions of the skies,
Skies than thyself ten times more impotent.
(Khayyam and Whinfield, 1980a, p. 66)

It can be argued that Khayyam did not believe in the same God preached by the religious establishment of his time. As Khayyam explained in his philosophical work, the only way to reconcile an omnipotent God and evil was to consider evil as the state of nonexistence, so it would not put God in a position of the creator of evil in this world. However, that position created a conundrum, as nonexistence would imply lacking temporality and consequently immutability because something in the state of nonexistence cannot change and therefore is immutable. This creates another dilemma. According to the orthodoxy of the time, an omnipotent God is not bounded by temporality and is in a state of perfection and needless of change. In other words, God is immutable, as the Westminster Shorter Catechism puts it: "[God] is a spirit, whose being, wisdom, power, holiness, justice, goodness, and truth are infinite, eternal, and unchangeable" (Muhling, 2020).

The problem with immutability is that it places God in the same category as Evil!

It is important to note that in Islam, immutability of holy words has been extended by some Muslims to other texts besides the Quran, including hadith (the majority of which compiled after the death of the prophet).

Extending the notion of immutability to words of the prophet and, as practiced in some branches of Islam, his successors (for instance, in Shiism) creates an insurmountable obstacle to reconcile time with religious practices.

> In you it is not one thing to be and another to live: the supreme degree of being and the supreme degree of life are one and the same thing. You are being in a supreme degree and are immutable. In you the present day has no ending, and yet in you it has its end: "all these things have their being in you" (Rom.11.36). They would have no way of passing away unless you set a limit to them. Because "your years do not fail" (Ps.101.28), your years are one Today. (Augustine, Confessions, I. vi (10))
> (Deng, 2018)

Those practices are impervious to the passage of time, demand nothing but absolute obedience. In other words, it is not a form of interaction but total surrender and conformity, treating their subjects as a flock.

As Dr. Charles Kimball puts it:

> Authentic religion engages the intellect as people wrestle with the mystery of existence and the challenges of living in an imperfect world. Conversely, blind obedience is a sure sign of a corrupt religion. Beware of any religious movement that seeks to limit the intellectual freedom and individual integrity of its adherents. When individual believers abdicate personal responsibility and yield to the authority of a charismatic leader or become enslaved to particular ideas or teachings, religion can easily become the framework for violence and destruction.
> (Kimball, 2002)

This is not the God that Khayyam portrays in his quartet. While in his philosophical work, he raises the question of evil and reconciles it with nonexistence, in his poetry, he speaks of the creator that is responsible for both good and evil in the world.

The secrets which my book of love has bred, Cannot be told for fear of loss of head; Since none is fit to learn, or cares to know,
Tis better all my thoughts remain unsaid.
                              (Khayyam and Tirtha, 1941, p. 266)

The good and evil with man's nature blent,
The weal and woe that heaven's decrees have sent,
Impute them not to motions of the skies,
Skies than thyself ten times more impotent.
                              (Khayyam and Whinfield, 1980b, p. 66)

Furthermore, Khayyam rebels against the notion of obedience and asceticism. Khayyam emphasizes interaction with the aesthetic aspect of life to appreciate the moments emerging from such exchange. Khayyam's poetry shows a preference for beauty and joy over blight and misery.

My law it is in pleasure's paths to stray,
My creed to shun the theologic fray;
I wedded Luck, and offered her a dower,
She said, "I want none, so thy heart be gay."
                              (Khayyam and Whinfield, 1980a, p. 40)

In contrast to orthodox jurists' immutable and timeless God, Khayyam's God is, at least in his poetry, human-centric. We seek truth and happiness in this world as it presents itself to us, be it nature, our body, mind, or feelings. It is up to us to choose between the beautiful and the ugly. We have a choice between being active and seeking what brings us joy and happiness versus being passive in being driven by habits and rituals. What is presented to us is a fundamental choice, deciding the path in our life, one that goes through skepticism acknowledging the falsifiability of our beliefs, the other is conforming to what is preached by the messengers of an immutable God and surrender to their certainty about their plan for the afterlife, one that requires sacrifices and suffering in this world in exchange for an eternal reward in changeless heaven.

> *How sweet is mortal Sovranty!"—think some:*
> *Others—"How blest the Paradise to come!"*
> *Ah, take the Cash in hand and waive the Rest;*
> *Oh, the brave Music of a distant Drum!*
> (Khayyam and FitzGerald, 1997)

Khayyam's choice of the immediate over the promised land is not a choice of now versus the future. It is foremost about having the will to choose this changing world and its temporality and reject the changeless and timeless afterlife.

> *As they without me run the Fortune's Plume,*
> *Then how to make this mate the charge assume?!*
> *Without me yore, today the same, the morn*
> *On what charges the Judge would rule my doom?*
> (Parchizadeh, 2010)

The only reality is our temporary temporal existence: the span of and space of this world that we have control over. Therefore, it is imperative to not listen to the Sufis or the Sheikhs, as they call to prayer, and Zekr is placing shackles on being in the short window of life.

The will to choose is fundamental for creativity, allowing the world to present itself to us, naturally and without the filter of dogmatic ideology, and choose to interact with its beauties and wonders, without prejudice but with curiosity and question.

> *To lovers true what matters, dark or fair*
> *In hell or heaven, love mates would not care Nor if a*
> *brick or bolster rest their heads*
> *Nor whether silk or serge Beloved does wear.*
> (Khayyam and Whinfield, 1980a)

The world of Sheikhs and Sufis has no questions or curiosity; they have answers and prescriptions. Khayyam stands against the changeless straitjacket of religious doctrine, as it is ill-suited to cope with his growing interest in knowledge.

> *Never was my hearth deprived of science*
> *Little mysteries remained unsolved*
> *From Dawn to dusk, for Seventy two years*
> *I contemplated*
> *Discovered at last, I know nothing.*[4]

What gives meaning and purpose to life is realizing this world's capacity for creative opportunity and fulfilling its potential to provide choice. Through the development of taste, one can enhance the quality of their subject of choice, like a sommelier (Merriam-Webster, 2020) appreciating a fine wine made by a master winemaker. Living in the creative moment is an artistic act; it demands making conscious choices about what and who to interact with, like pairing food; it involves taste and requires intellectual interrogation.

> *O friend! let us not worry about tomorrow*
> *seize the brief life*
> *tomorrow we depart this transient world*
> *to company those went seven thousand years.*[5]

Eschewing the fantasy of the afterlife in favor of the harsh reality of the present is essential to understand the reality of life in this world and find purpose by enriching its moments. The art of living is not only finding the value of its moment but integrating them, like a maestro conducting a symphony orchestra, where every instrument and their play are an essential element in the creative experience.

> *Behind the curtain none has found his way None came to know the secret as we could say*

And each repeats the dirge his fancy taught Which has no sense—but never ends the lay.
(Tirtha and Khayyam, 1941, p. 229)

The question is, where should we draw the purpose of life? What gives meaning to our time on this earth? Is it achieved through carrying the prescribed scripture of the religious authority and reaching uniformity and salvation?

But what is the cause of the harm that necessitates salvation? The Encyclopedia Britannica defines salvation in religion as the deliverance of humankind from such fundamentally adverse or disabling conditions as suffering, evil, finitude, and death. (Brandon, 2017).

But to believe in something that cannot be proven rationally means that our trust and belief system has to be debased, from reason to a method of unverifiable metaphors.

To drain the cup, to hover round the fair
Can hypocrite's art with these compare?
If all who love and drink are bound for hell
There is many a Wight of heaven may well dear.
(Whinfield, 2013, p. 256)

What is the price of reaching eternal life and happiness, or if such a notion is even possible or desirable? According to Khayyam, at least in his poetry, the afterlife is nothing more than a myth, as there is no direct human experience possible, and it instead belongs to the realm of faith.

Who e'er returned of all that went before,
To tell of that long road they travel o'er?
Leave naught undone of what you have to do,
For when you go, you will return no more.
(Khayyam and Whinfield, 1980b, p. 174)

Rubaiyat portraits life as an experience in contrast, the capacity to do evil and good embedded in our unconscious. We have a choice to make, to be creative or be an imitator, to look at the mysteries of the universe through the lens of rationality, or procrastinate its answers to the promise of tomorrow.

> *The good or evil human nature moulds,*
> *And bliss or bane which He in power unfolds,*
> *Are not from stars. The stars in path of love*
> *Are meeker far than man who thinks and scolds.*
>   (Tirtha and Khayyam, 1941, p. 28)

The choice of beauty and joy is not only liberating, but it brings responsibility, as the call to "seize the moment and enjoy life with cheers" invokes one's free will to make a conscious choice. In other words, life is not an imitation of the divine plan but a canvas with the exponential expanse of imagination.

> *Thy nature's knit by breath or fancies frail,*
> *Be just not harsh to people that they ail*
> *Sit thou with wise and see that I and thou*
> *Is grain of dust, a spark, a drop and gale.*
>   (Tirtha and Khayyam, 1941, p. 90)

Rubaiyat is the work of a poet, philosopher, and mathematician who demonstrates what cannot be explained mathematically or reconciled philosophically can be composed and interpreted artistically. The seeming contradiction between Khayyam's philosophical work and the Rubaiyat is caused by missing his intellectual standing as a freethinker and an artist. Khayyam's philosophical work on the question of the afterlife is notable; however, as a scientist like many preceding him, he knew well that it could not be proved or rejected logically.

It is noteworthy that belief in the afterlife is an escape from nonexistence and the responsibility to face the real cause of life's suffering. Afterlife, where one is rewarded or punished on the basis of their performance in life, as prescribed by the religious establishment, is a distraction from the cause of pain and misery in life. In other words, escape from nonexistence results in ignoring the will and logic to become the subject of a narrative set by the guardians of the religion.

As Stewart Guthrie points out, humans tend to attribute human characteristics to nonhuman events (Guthrie, 2008), and belief in the afterlife can be explained as a measure of risk mitigation in the face of grave punishment for nonbelievers

> The cost of false positives—such as thinking that a coiled rope is a snake at first glance—is very low, resulting in a mere shock. But the result of a false negative—thinking that a snake is a rope—can cost you everything in biological terms.
>
> (Guthrie, 1993)

> *Nor you nor I can read the etern decree,*
> *To that enigma we can find no key;*
> *They talk of you and me behind the veil,*
> *But, if that veil be lifted, where are we?*
> (Khayyam and Whinfield, 1980a, p. 260)

While the allure of endless bounties in a different life can be captivating, it has a debilitating effect on improving human conditions. Unlike the economy, where frugality and waiving or spending the present for the benefit of future growth is considered a path to prosperity, postponing living in the moment brings nothing but regret in the future.

> *Today is thine to spend, but not to-morrow,*
> *Counting on morrow breedeth naught but sorrow;*
> *Oh! Squander not this breath that heaven hath lent thee,*
> *Nor make too sure another breath to borrow.*
> (Khayyam and Whinfield, 1980a)

Living in the moment is an act of art, as it involves connecting and interacting with others and the world. It requires intention and effort to understand, ask questions, and move boundaries of established beliefs and social arrangements. Being in the moment involves the practice of attention to deficiencies and hidden complexities, and deliberately creative acts of reanimation, from passivity and seclusion. It is an educative effort to sharpen the consciousness and drive the imagination and to be able to look at what is possible rather than being content with what is granted to us. It is being engrossed with life and its possibilities, not to forget death, but to accept it and see it as a life dimension. Being in the moment is an act of liberation from conforming forces of established social powers. In other words, being in the moment is, as Nietzsche put it, overcoming a reactive state and becoming active.

> Consciousness represents and recognises active forces, thereby separating activity from what it can do. Such separation constitutes a subtraction or division of active force by making it work against the power of its own affirmation. The remarkable feature of the becoming-reactive of active force is that historically it has managed to form the basis of an entire vision of life. This vision embodies the principle of "ressentiment": a movement in which a reactive and resentful denial of higher life begins to create its own moral system and account of human experience. The reactive triumph expressed in movements of consciousness like ressentiment, bad consciousness and the ascetic ideal depends upon a mystification and reversal of active force: at the core of these new interpretations of life, reactive force simulates active force and turns it against itself. It is at precisely the historical moment when the slave begins to triumph over the master who has stopped being the spectre of law, virtue, morality, and religion.
>
> (Spinks, 2010)

While Khayyam expresses a sense of powerlessness in the face of death, he appreciates the value of the moment and the aesthetic aspect of life as the only worthy cause of life. There are similarities between the two, as in *Thus Spoke Zarathustra* Nietzsche writes:

> do not believe those who speak to you of otherworldly hopes! Poison mixers are they, whether they know it or not. Despisers of life are they, decaying and poisoned themselves, of whom the earth is weary: so let them go.
> (Nietzsche and Kaufmann, 1978)

Khayyam's message, preceding Nietzsche by eight centuries, resonates:

In a lone waste I saw a debauchee, He had no home, no faith, no heresy,
No God, no truth, no law, no certitude
Where in this World is man so bold as he?
(Khayyam and Whinfield, 1980b, p. 252)

Abandoning the myth of the afterlife was not only a courageous act but, given the intolerance of the established religious orthodoxy, a dangerous one. At that time, being a philosopher was enough to put one in harm's way.

My critics call me a philosopher,
But God knows full well they greatly err; I know not even what I am, much less
Why on this earth I am a sojourner.
(Khayyam and Whinfield, 1980b, p. 234)

The secrets which my book of love has bred,
Cannot be told for fear of loss of head;
Since none is fit to learn, or cares to know,
'Tis better all my thoughts remain unsaid.
(Tirtha and Khayyam, 1941, p. 266)

While deflecting the blame of being a philosopher, Khayyam clearly expresses his commitment to the essence of philosophy, questioning our existence. This act of questioning is the foundation of philosophy. It allows us to think about concepts such as being and becoming, existence and reality, and knowledge and ways it is acquired.

Like all scholars and intellectuals, Khayyam valued his freedom of thought and used the power of poetry, philosophy, and science to preserve his freedom of thought and expand his creative space. Providing his service to the rulers' court offered him protection from the continuous assault of traditional Islamic jurists who despised his rationalist worldview. His insistence on defending his freedom and perhaps his life compelled him to embark on a long journey to Mecca to prove his piety and avoid persecution.

Khayyam's lack of attachment to a location seemed from his commitment to his creative space, as his ideas and freedom of thought dictated where he lived and whom he worked for, not the other way around.

In that respect, he was similar to many contemporary freethinkers and intellectuals, moving across continents to find a haven where they can not only be able to work freely but, most importantly, be inspired to expand their creativity and possibilities.

Khayyam was an outlier, thinking outside the realm of established orthodoxy preached by the Islamic jurists of his time. What they preached was a strict reading of the scripture. Approval from religious authority was essential for the rulers to maintain their legitimacy in the populace's eye. This symbiotic relationship dated back to Iran's pre-Arab invasion and was reestablished soon after Arab rulers were introduced to the Persian elites' rule of governance. However, Khayyam was meticulous in his approach to the ignorance and intolerance of the establishment. On the one hand, he was careful not to be labeled as an infidel, which could cost him his head, and on the other hand, he was careful to preserve his intellectual integrity and not subjugate himself to the banality of superstitious beliefs and practices.

His poetry is the best source and proof of his struggle to create the protection for his creative space while allowing him to shed light on the meaninglessness of repetitive rituals that dictated and limited imagination and creativity.

What was paramount to Khayyam was the preservation and expansion of his imaginative mind, where he could contemplate the secrets of the universe and appreciate the beauty of the cosmos as it presented itself to him. Khayyam recognized prejudice and dated dogmas as the most prominent veils that obscured the world's beauty and harmony. His approach to the universe was neither mystical nor mired by religious superstition. He was genuinely committed to empirical evidence and aware of the limit and inadequacy of human knowledge.

It can be argued that what mattered to Khayyam was the pursuit of knowledge, as he saw the time best spent as being aware of the temporal nature of our being and finding remedies to enrich it.

Some have argued that he was a hedonist advocating, spending time drinking wine, and philandering. However, that would be a rather superficial reading of his poetry. One has to see his poetry following his philosophical and scientific work while considering his era's social conditions and context.

> *At first they brought me perplexed in this way, Amazement still enhances day by day;*
> *We all alike are tasked to go, but Oh!*
> *Why are we brought and sent? This none can say.*
> (Khayyam and Whinfield, 1980a, p. 18)

Among scientists who have changed our perspective of time, Albert Einstein is the most prominent one. Einstein revolutionized our understanding of time and space. According to Einstein's theory of relativity, time is measured according to the observer's frame of reference (Geroch, 1981). That implies that there is no universal measurement of time. For instance, if we send one twin on a space journey for a year traveling close to the speed of light, the other twin would be a few years older by the time they would come back to the earth. While time is measured according to the observer's frame of reference, life's frame of reference consists of beliefs and worldviews that use the past, present, and future.

To put it differently, we live in the present while thinking of the past and contemplating the future. Future provides the potential and the possibility that depends on an action performed in the present, an act that can be informed by the past's memory. Placing life's frame of reference in the present is vital in the Khayyamian worldview.

While Einstein's theory provides rules about the flow of time, it does not explain the present's meaning. Rudolf Carnap explains Einstein's dilemma (Carnap, 1963, pp. 37–38):

> Once Einstein said that the problem of the Now worried him seriously. He explained that the experience of the Now means something special for man, something essentially different from the past and the future, but that this important difference does not and cannot occur within physics. That this experience cannot be grasped by science seemed to him a matter of painful but inevitable resignation. I remarked that all that occurs objectively can be described in science; on the one hand, the temporal sequence of events is described in physics; and, on the other hand, the peculiarities of man's experiences concerning time, including his different attitude towards past, present, and future, can be described and (in principle) explained in psychology. But Einstein thought that these scientific descriptions could not possibly satisfy our human needs; there is something essential about the Now, which is just outside the realm of science. We both agreed that this was not a question of a defect for which science could be blamed, as Bergson thought. I did not wish to press the point because I wanted to primarily understand his attitude to the problem rather than clarify the theoretical situation. But I had the impression that Einstein's thinking on this point involved a lack of distinction between experience and knowledge. Since science in

principle can say all that can be said, there is no unanswerable question left. But though there is no theoretical question left, there is still the common human emotional experience, which is sometimes disturbing for special psychological reasons.

(Carnap, 1963)

While physical rules cannot explain the meaning of the Now, art transcends both time and space to create its frame of reference, anchored in expanded creative space. Its coordinates are anchored in displaced beliefs and transformed social boundaries.

The flow of time in the physical realm follows its rule; according to the theory of relativity, one cannot be simultaneously in the present, past, and future; however, art transcends time. The artistic view of the present and nowness, being in the moment, transcends time and space as it can reach into the past while discovering the future. While a physical system can predict its future, it cannot contemplate its condition outside its possible states. Art inventiveness not only creates possibilities but connects and collapses the flow of time to create the opportunity of enpresenting, making things present in the present (Dreyfus and Wrathall, 2002).

Art has the unique capability of summoning the spirit of the past and future aspirations to enrich and expand the space-time of the present. The present is pregnant with possibilities that need to be revealed, and art has the power of presenting the present, burdened with the past and pregnant with the future.

The other towering figure of twentieth century who has transformed our knowledge of time is Stephen Hawking, who proposed that the big bang was the origin of time (Dasch and O'Meara, 2018) he states: "I think the universe was spontaneously created out of nothing according to the laws of science." The idea of the spontaneous creation of the universe has been debated for a long time among physicists and philosophers alike. Nothingness contains infinite possibilities, as it is not bounded or regulated by the condition of existence. In other words, nothingness is pregnant with limitless potential. Such potential itself, according to the quantum theory, gives rise to the creation of the universe (Gleiser, 2013).

Khayyam addresses it elegantly:

> *Since naught we hold in hand of ought but air,*
> *Since ought in hand is but of vain affair,*
> *Presume it aught: what thou perceive is not!*
> *Assume it naught: what thou conceive is there!*
>
> (Parchizadeh, 2010)

Khayyam sees any moment in life as a creative space, a source of possibilities bounded only by our choices. In other words, a meaningful life is the integration of its creative moments. At the same time, bonded by birth and death, it has the potential for unlimited possibilities, regulated only by the choices we make.

In the Khayyam worldview, moments are the concentration of the past, the present, and the future; it contains all that there is in life, the path to happiness goes through grasping the moment and be present to its content.

Moments like a fine wine are a concentration of all that brought it to us, waiting to be uncorked, paired, and accompanied to create joy.

It is essential to note the prominent role of wine in Khayyam poetry. It is not an instrument of forgetfulness, as Khayyam's definition of joy is far from a drunken stupor. Wine is a concentration of time and space; probably no other product of humans carries so much meaning as wine. Wine brings the smell and character of the soil that vine roots explored and spread in; it carries the fairness of the air and the wind that caress the grapes, the water that quenched its thirst, and the caring hands of the orchard lord. All cultivated, preserved, and cared for to transcribe the time and history in its flavor, texture, and taste. By the time it arrives at the hand of Khayyam, it joyfully expands the creative space of mind, probably expressed itself as a mathematical expression, as it is an integration of moments of life in the passage of time.

THE CREATIVE SPACE

Wine can be considered the finest concentrations of artisan tradition, time, and the earth's bounties. Like art, wine has no telos; its duty is not reconciling philosophical positions nor balancing the scientific equation but to tell a story of time and places, and of the toil of the wine master.

To understand Khayyam's appreciation of wine, one must look at the grape's journey from the ground to the jar in ancient Persia.

Ancient Persia was one of the first places where winemaking as a craft was invented. Archaeological investigations have shown that it was in Persia that the earliest wine was made in world history. [2] At Godin Tepe in Western Persia, the earliest evidence for winemaking and wine points to the fourth millennium BCE.

Wine played an essential role in the social hierarchy and was mentioned in the royal food menu for Persian Kings during the Sasanid era (224–651 CE), as stated in (King) Husraw and Page, a Middle Persian text from the Sasanian Empire (224–651 CE) (Daryaee, 2020).

> May you be immortal, these wines are all good and fine, the wine of Transoxania, when they prepare it well, the wine of Herat, the wine of Marw-Rud, the wine of Bust and the must of Hulwan, but no wine can ever compare with the Babylonian wine and the must of Bazrang.
> (Insler, 1975)

That is probably the first written wine recommendation by a wine connoisseur.

Touraj Daryaee (2020), in "Wine good and fine The art of wine in ancient Persia," gives an account of the importance of wine in Persian culture and history:

> It is with the first Persian dynasty, the Achaemenid Empire (550–330 BCE), that we find the culture of wine drinking in the form of long drinking vessels known as rhython. We hear that the Persian court was most elaborate place of feasting that the Greeks knew. The existence of rhytons and the mention of wine filters

(Greek oino th toi) in the antique literature from Persia, all suggest the importance of the drink.

He continues with Herodotus description of wine in Persian culture:

> Herodotus tells us that the Persians were very [fond] of wine (Old Persoan batu) and that they made important decisions in the following manner. First they became drunk, since they believed that only when you are drunk do you tell the truth. Then, the next day when they were sober they reconsidered the matter.[6] Pliny states that wine was also used with drugs for collecting information. The type of drug used with wine was called Achaemenis which had the following effect: "when it is drunk in wine, criminals confess to everything."
>
> (Daryaee, 2020)

He provides an essential source for wine classification and its characteristics:

> This interest in wine in Ancient Persia is manifest not only in material culture such as jars, plates and cups but is also documented in the written sources.
>
> [(King) Husraw and Page] was composed at the court of the King of Kings, Khosraw I in the sixth century CE, one of the greatest of the Sasanian monarchs who ruled Persia. What this text demonstrates that, just as today when we identify wines with regions such as France, Australia, Italy, California, etc. the Persians also were interested in wines from all regions. By this time the various kinds of wines were distinguished, by their color and filtering technique.
>
> The taste for various wines included may i sepid "white wine," may i suxr "red wine." These wines if course could have different qualities such as may i wirastag "clarified

wine," or also badag i abgen "crystal wine," which were served in dolag or tong. For information on the daily usage and consumption of wine we can look at the papyri which are basically letters between Persian officers in the seventh century CE and which mention the following (Papyri 8809).

(Daryaee, 2020)

Islam's ban on consumption of alcoholic beverages did not stop wine from being an essential part of everyday life and a powerful Persian literature aspect, both literally and metaphorically.

The world's a cipher Here's a cipher mine
I only think of love and lucid Wine,
They say, May He avert thee from thy Wine,
He won't, and if He would, then I resign.
(Khayyam and Tirtha, 1941, p. 245)

Khayyam's worldview provides a path to living life artistically; Khayyam's way of life was a confluence of rationality and artistic rebellion. His reality is an artistic reflection of rationality in consciousness.

While Physics struggles to explain the nowness, art provides an answer. The present is the window of creativity, an opportunity to bring the past and future together. Life can be considered a book, where the present is the blank page to be written using the vocabulary provided by history; the heritage and future are possibilities waiting to be unlocked by our choice and imagination; and the present is the intersection of past and the future. In this worldview, we choose what goes on each page. Many write and rewrite dictée on echoes of the past, filling their pages with repetition, creating endless loops where imagination is paralyzed and creativity is condemned. Others leave it blank, living as a predictable cog of modern machinery; their notebook is an operating manual, typed by the machinery they are tasked to operate.

Art provides salvation from certitude. Only through the unbounded capacity of art can possible and impossible be framed together. Being Artisan is the process of transcending borders and limits. It is boundless yet individual, not matching the scale of institutionalized beliefs and systems, yet dwarfing them in ideas and possibilities.

Where we depart from art, our reality becomes distorted, simplistic, and pedestrian, devoid of its complexities and hidden layers. Choosing to live with beauty is not motivated by hedonism; it is the supreme act of rebellion against the enslaving power of uniformity and homogeneity.

Notes

1 Translated by the author.
2 Translated by the author.
3 Translated by the author.
4 Translated by the author.
5 Translated by the author.

3
LIFE AS INTEGRATION OF MOMENTS

Khayyam coupled a methodical approach to the questions of existence and rational interrogation of the norms and traditions of the day with an authentic artistic streak, which provided him a shield against the intrusion of the dogmatic religious establishment. While Khayyam's work in math and philosophy can be compared to many post-renaissance thinkers and intellectuals, his approach set him apart. While pursuing his scientific and philosophical project, he deflects the accusation of being philosophical, a dangerous allegation, in particular at the time of tyrannical religious domination.

To understand the extent of Khayyam's struggle against the religious establishment, one has to consider the structure of the power and the society at that time.

No one is more notable as an obstacle to Khayyam's way of thought in the 11th century than Abu Hammid Ghazali. Ghazali's rebuttal of Greeks philosophy tradition and Avi Sina, who Khayyam revered, set the course for the domination of strict and ultra-orthodox interpretation of the scripture. Ghazali's method forbade rationalist tradition and opposed skepticism and a philosophical approach to the questions of being and existence.

Many argue that the decline of science in the Islamic world started with the domination of such a worldview. For Khayyam, the dominance of orthodox jurists meant that he had to make a hard choice; either choose a path of easy life and living peacefully by subjugating to the tradition or dare to question the status quo and oppose the established beliefs and risk his life. The former would mean being forgotten over time while the latter would guarantee his place in the history.

Khayyam's approach to the dogmatic worldviews of Ghazali was to employ, masterfully, the nuances of the Persian language by poetically encoding his intellectual and philosophical positions. As a mathematician, his use of words for his quartets is quite precise. While at the surface, they might be interpreted as advocating for just having a good time, they reveal a much deeper and more complex message, one that shows the author's commitment to a rational way of life. Khayyam sees time as one of the most valuable assets in our life, which should only be spent pursuing creative happiness. It is important to note that Khayyam's interpretation of happiness is not spending his life as a drunkard and womanizer but finding meaning through creativity and excellence.

Khayyam's commitment to his intellectual work required freedom of thought, which was only possible by avoiding the prevalent herd mentality. He ridiculed and showed the banality of the masses and their corrupting influence on human intellect.

> *In heaven is seen the bull we name Parwln,*
> *Beneath the earth another lurks unseen*
> *And thus to wisdom's eyes humanity appear*
> *A drove of asses, two great bulls between.*
>
> (Whinfield, 2013, p. 252)

Khayyam's view was in contrast to Al-Ghazali, who frowned upon finding happiness in earthly matters and saw salvation in one's dedication to metaphysics of afterlife, believing in immutable laws set by the prophet for all humankind, impervious to the changing world and circumstances of its human subjects.

Khayyam's path to happiness goes through this world and does not veer into the mirage of the afterlife. His poem does not portray an angry God, who is bent on revenging their worldly sins with the eternal flame of hell despite his might and power over the path for his creatures. Khayyam depicts hell and paradise as absurdities, nonsensical promises that distract us from the moment, in particular, and consequently the life itself. Distraction from the moment, here and now, makes us lose sight of life and all that is beautiful and present. Distraction from newness would lead to loss of sense of self and individuality, or as Khayyam calls it, becoming the donkeys between Oxen in the Sky and the earth.

> *Did He who made me fashion me for hell,*
> *Or destine me for heaven? I can not tell.*
> *... Yet will I not renounce cup, lute, and love,*
> *Nor earthly cash for heavenly credit sell.*
> (Whinfield, 2013, p. 64)

Khayyam's message of maximizing earthly happiness stands in contrast to Ghazali's advocacy for restraints and asceticism. Khayyam's path to happiness is not through drinking and promiscuity but the commitment to understanding life and being mindful of the opportunity it presents to us. Fulfilling the moment is achieved by renewing our values and becoming different in thinking and living. Becoming free requires breaking the restraints of dogma and banal traditions.

It can be argued that his intellectual project made him a dedicated advocate of individuation, believing that freedom can only be achieved by freeing oneself from the homogeneity of the masses and questioning our existence. Khayyam's insistence on valuing moments meant that he saw life as an integration of its moments. While many consider mathematics as a tool of computation, to Khayyam, it was a source of inspiration and meaning.

He applied math in his science and questioned the very axioms that were the foundation of mathematics. It is essential to understand the importance of mathematics in Khayyam's worldview; Khayyam challenged the axiomatic foundation of the Euclidian geometry (Boyer, 1988), in particular, the universality of parallel lines; it is argued that his elaborate attempt to prove the parallel postulate was significant, as they provided the first theorems for development of non-Euclidean geometries (Rashid and Vahabzadeh, 2000).

According to Rosenfeld and Youschkevitch (1973), "by placing irrational quantities and numbers on the same operational scale, [Khayyam] began a true revolution in the doctrine of number" (Struik, 1958).

Khayyam's bold attempt to challenge the foundation of mathematics may explain his approach in his philosophy and art. Were Khayyam's poems a camouflage for his steadfast belief and philosophical positions? That is plausible since Khayyam, the mathematicians, had no tolerance of dogma and staying within the framework set by his predecessors. In both his scientific work and poetry, he demonstrated freethinking and disrupted the accepted norms of the day.

> the work of Omar Khayyam in the 12th century in solving algebraic equations and describe how his work may have influenced René Descartes in the 17th century. In particular, we discuss his solutions of cubic equations; these equations absorbed mathematicians from 9th to 16th century. Omar made a significant contribution to the finding of positive root through geometrical argument and thus foreshadowed the analytical geometry of Descartes.
>
> (Mardia, 2004)

Khayyam's work on Euclid's fifth postulate, accurately demonstrating that it could not be derived from the other four, was groundbreaking for his era and was ahead of his time by many centuries. Khayyam's work in developing methods for describing objects with more than three dimensions was necessary to understand space-time.

By pioneering the application of algebraic equations to geometry, Khayyam started a revolution in mathematics that paved the road to analytic geometry, which saw application in science, engineering, and space exploration (Khayyam, 1070).[1]

LIFE AS INTEGRATION OF MOMENTS

Khayyam brought the same analytical approach to the question of existence; for him, freedom meant the ability to look at the world from a skeptical perspective. He was an enthusiastic believer in the incompleteness of our knowledge,

Never from worldly toils have I been free,
Never for one short moment glad to be!
I served a long apprenticeship to fate,
But yet of fortune gained no mastery.

(Tirtha and Khayyam, 1941, p. 232)

The question remains that how is that someone so committed to his scientific work and rationality can be an ardent advocate of drinking wine. As some have argued, is Khayyam's wine a mystical reference to God or as others have proposed, a sign of his hedonistic worldview?

To understand Khayyam's position on this matter, one has to look at his life in balance. There is little doubt that Khayyam enjoyed drinking good wine, but not in quantities that would prevent his sharp mind from engaging with his scientific work.

Drink wine with the wise
Or enjoy it with a smiling beauty
Avoid excess, lest revealing secrets
A sip, on occasion, and discreetly.[2]

(Foroughi, 1976)

Indeed he might have enjoyed wine like many other intellectuals to reduce the tension of dealing with dogmatic orthodoxies of the day and expand his emotional and creative space. As known to artists and authors, wine could be a good company when consumed in moderation. Khayyam, too, was prescribing wine as an occasional sip to enrich the moment and deepen our sense of life.

For Khayyam, wine is not an elixir to the world of forgetfulness and mystical fantasies but the realization of the real sense of being in the present, expanding the moment and what possibilities it can bring about. To him, drinking wine is an act

LIFE AS INTEGRATION OF MOMENTS

of awakening from mediocrity. Khayyam's wine sharpens the thought and eases the words, freely expressing his thought's harmony.

But why wine and no other material enjoyment? What is special about wine to make it a reoccurring theme in Khayyam poetry. Was it because of the old proverb *oinon kai aletheia* (or in vino veritas) that wine brings the truth out? To better understand Khayyam's love of wine, one should look at winemaking's creative ingredients: good grapes, knowledge, commitment, and time. When a bottle of fine wine is poured, it conveys more than an enjoyable drink. It becomes a narrator of history, culture, and tradition. It tells a story about soil and air, the loving labor of the vineyard master, and above all, the past it has witnessed. It is the concentration of time and space, combining all elements of life in its texture, taste, and potency; in other words, it is a book of time.

Khayyam's reference to wine is often literal. Wine brings history to the present, enriching and expanding it. Its connection with time is profound; there is no other product with the same quality of the wine, combining and delivering many aspects and qualities of life with such potency. Suppose a clock shows the passage of time, wine witnesses it. In many aspects, it is like a living being, starting its journey as a grape, growing and becoming complete through the passage of time and proper care of the artisan winemaker. Passage of time leaves distinct and recognizable marks on its character, texture, taste, and aroma. It can tell us when and where it was made and the quality of its ingredient. The acting of popping the bottle is like opening a time capsule; it invites us to expand our horizons and open our eyes to the moment. In other words, it is an integration of time and life.

Wine is not only a storyteller. It can also liberate and sharpen the thought, focusing it on the moments and highlighting its possibilities, bringing the past and the future to the present. Wine is honest, as in contrast with the promissory nature of piety; it delivers its liberating force promptly, expanding space and time through the potent power of life itself.

LIFE AS INTEGRATION OF MOMENTS

Khayyam's reference to wine can be considered euphoric. His reference to wine is often accompanied by being present to the passage of time and life. Rather than becoming forgetful and drunk, Khayyam advocates expanding our view exploring the possibilities arising from the sharpened senses. To experience the liberating potency of wine, one must learn drinking etiquette, drink to become aware, not to forget.

What wine can bring to us is the revealing force that has the potential to open our eyes and allows the world to present itself as it is. No question, drinking wine in the era of orthodox jurists was an act of rebellion. It was an act of resistance against timelessness and loss of ability to evolve, change, and progress through time. Religious establishment advocated an immutable world where humans were merely conforming to predetermined shapes; every step they took was delivering the will of their creator, like the puppet in the hand of the puppeteer.

This doctrine left little room for imagination and creativity. An immutable world and its masters have little tolerance and mercy on outliers and people who think or act out of the narrow margins of traditions.

As Bruce Lee, the martial artist, philosopher, and filmmaker, points out:

> We have more faith in what we imitate than in what we originate. We cannot derive a sense of absolute certitude from anything that has its roots in us. The most poignant sense of insecurity comes from standing alone; we are not alone when we imitate. It is thus with most of us! We are what other people say we are. We know ourselves chiefly by hearsay.
>
> (Lee, 2001)

On the subject of dogma and personal responsibility, Lee continues:

> There is a powerful craving in most of us to see ourselves as instruments in the hands of others and thus

free ourselves from the responsibility for acts that are prompted by our questionable inclinations and impulses. Both the strong and the weak grasp at the alibi. The latter hide their malevolence under the virtue of obedience; they acted dishonorably because they had to obey orders. The strong, too, claim absolution by proclaiming themselves the chosen instrument of a higher power—God, history, fate, nation, or humanity.
(Lee, 2001)

All guardians of different sect promised that their narrow path is the best and often only way to reach the imaginary almighty. Their preachers have made transporting humans to the imaginary heaven into a lucrative business.

Khayyam positioned his intellectual standing between the two dominant schools of thought of the day: on one side were the Islamic jurist's Puritan orthodoxies and on the other were the Sufis. While each side had their differences, both consider their teaching as the single path to truth and do not place much value on the earthly human condition, instead of seeking fulfillment in the metaphysical world, governed by the invisible and deterministic hand of an almighty creator.

The Islamic jurist and Sufis dominance over the intellectual discourse of the time acted as two sides of scissors, leaving little room for the skepticism and rationality of Khayyam.

Khayyam rebelled against this immutable view of the world when thinking philosophically was considered an act of heresy.

> *My enemies call me a philosopher,*
> *But God knows full well they greatly err;*
> *I know not even what I am, much less*
> *Why on this earth I am a sojourner.*
> (Khayyam and Whinfield, 1980a, p. 235)

While religious establishment promoted an invariable world, Sufism, a mystical belief and practice that grew out of early Islamic asceticism, advocated for the abdication of all worldly desire and to dissolve one in the love of God. It developed in reaction to the increasing worldliness of the Islamic society and the Ommayad period. *al-Ḥusayn ibn* Manṣūr al-Ḥallāj, who is a significant figure in Sufism, adopts the notion of "I'm God" (Fiegenbaum, 2018); in his view, he was the reflection of the God, which is often interpreted as a view that reality is identical with divinity (Pearsall, 1998). Ḥallāj lost his life over his beliefs and teaching, his death has been dramatized, and his image idolized through Persian Poems' work, particularly Rumi. He is often referred to as the "martyr of Love" (Shepard, 2021).

Sufism commanded a significant influence on Persian culture and art. In particular poetry, many great Persian-speaking poets advocate Sufism values and adhere to their tradition, particularly abstinence, accepting suffering to reach unity with God, and rejection of reason as a path to him. However, one interesting aspect of Persian poetry is wine as a metaphor for the ecstasy experienced by achieving different stages of the spiritual journey.

While Sufism and the Puritan school of thought were at odds, going as far as declaring Sufism polytheistic, both were united in their opposition to the values Khayyam stood for.

Khayyam rejects Sufism and its approach to life and God. As a rationalist, he believed in creating an understanding of the world through science and experiment, which put him at odds with Sufism's teaching, particularly their rejection of rationality as a path to reach God. It is important to note that Rumi, the most prominent Sufis poet, is revered by many in Iran. His work, Masnavi, is second only to Koran, which clearly shows the obstacle in challenging the Sufism worldview.

Khayyam did not believe in abstinence, though on the question of free will, he advocated a complex framework where free will exists within the sociopolitical structure

> *At first they brought me perplexed in this way*
> *Amazement still enhances day by day*
> *We all alike are tasked to go but Oh!*
> *Why are we brought and sent? This none can say.*
> (Tirtha and Khayyam, 1941, p. 18)

His poetry demonstrates the trait of Epicurean agnosticism, while in his philosophy, he shows commitment to God. How to explain this duality? Was Khayyam a true believer in a deterministic God, leaving no room for humans outside their predetermined path, or was he a firm individualist and free will advocate, as some of his poetry shows.

> *Tho' fount of joy, we are the source of sores,*
> *Tho' justice courts, we court the brutal force;*
> *We are the depths and heights, the parts and whole,*
> *We reflect Truth, but now we rust of course.*
>
> (Tirtha and Khayyam, 1941, p. 130)

Here again, Khayyam challenges conventional thinking; while showing his amazement of the universe's complexities, he proposes hard questions about the nature of our existence. As a scientist, he firmly believes in a rationalist view of the world, but at the same time, he recognized and described the awe and bewilderment of our existence in his poetry.

While this duality might seem confusing, it demonstrates Khayyam's ability to propose different approaches dealing with multiple facets of our lives. Even though our position in the universe, as creatures dwelling on the earth, is determined by cosmic bodies' movement,[3] our happiness results from our wisdom.

> *Me thinks this celestial wheel*
> *at which we gape and stare,*
> *Is Chinese lantern-like we buy at fair;*
> *The lamp is Sun, and paper-shade the world,*
> *And we the pictures whirling unaware.*
>
> (Tirtha and Khayyam, 1941, p. 17)

> *The good and evil with man's nature blent,*
> *The weal and woe that heaven's decrees have sent,—*
> *Impute them not to motions of the skies,—*
> *Skies than thyself ten times more impotent.*
>
> (Khayyam and Whinfield, 1980a, p. 66)

Jalali calendar was invented using scientific and accurate methods using astronomical observations and mathematical calculation. Jalali calendar invention played an essential role in religious rituals and separation of religious calendar (which is lunar-based) from state calendar (Jalai calendar and its derivatives are solar-based), effectively rationalizing state chronology and separating it from sacred ritual cycles. This effort happened when rationalism was under attack by Islamic jurists. However, Khayyam's response to intellectual strangulation is brilliant. He placed the divine order in a mathematical framework through his scientific work, devising a calendar based on mathematically calibrated cosmological observation, thus, paving the way for the ultimate subjugation of religion by science.

To understand Khayyam's stand against the immutability of religious orthodoxy, one has to focus on the concept of time, as seen through Khayyam's work. Khayyam's philosophical work delves deep into the subject of free will, determinism, and life and death. The fascinating aspect of his character is that while, as a philosopher, he ponders on cosmological determinism, Khayyam, the poet, questions the afterlife and concentrates on nowness and choice. The contradiction between his philosophical position and his poetry has led some to question his poetry's authenticity; however, they make sense if paying attention to Khayyam's use of poetry to expand the creative space and challenge beliefs beyond the reach of science and reason.

Khayyam, the philosopher, poses serious existential questions and tries to answer them based on available knowledge. Is this world predestined? Do humans have free will? Is there a life after death? On the other hand, Khayyam, the poet, challenges the very same positions. By doing so, Khayyam places himself at the intersection of art and science. In his science, he rigorously pursues knowledge, not shying from upending standard views of the scientific and religious establishment. In his artistic work, he confesses to the incompleteness of our expertise and advocates for realizing the value of our time.

LIFE AS INTEGRATION OF MOMENTS

Whilom, ere youth's conceit had waned, me- thought
Answers to all life's problems I had wrought;
But now, grown old and wise, too late I see
My life is spent, and all my lore is naught.

(Khayyam and Whinfield, 1980a, p. 96)

If misunderstood, his work could look like a disparate collage of different positions, going as far as creating doubt about the authenticity of some of his poems. However, when considered in balance, it makes sense. Khayyam creates his own creative space by showing us how to liberate ourselves from the confines of traditions and history. In other words, through his way of life, he teaches us how to liberate time. What comes next is our choice.

The good and evil with man's nature blent,
The weal and woe that heaven's decrees have sent,
Impute them not to motions of the skies,
Skies than thyself ten times more impotent.

(Khayyam and Whinfield, 1980a, p. 66)

Religious dogma implants its followers with immutable ceremonies. The cosmos cycles are substituted with ritualistic practices, claimed to be sent from a metaphysical world inaccessible to all but saints and prophets. These rituals greatly diminish our sovereignty over our daily lives. Most importantly, they replace the concept of life as an integration of moments with an eternal procession where humans are subject to their creator's will, acting as a cast in a play where the narrative has been adopted and their role predetermined. Their act is to participate as their role calls for, looping through the rituals in the hope of promissory salvation in the afterlife.

Khayyam's position on life and what gives meaning to it is in contrast with this view, reminding us of the moment which is an invitation to revolt against the serfdom and to liberate oneself from the meaningless mirage. The nowness is to focus and enrich what is available to us, see the world as it presents itself, and experience togetherness. In other words, Khayyam advocates for throwing away the false implants of the past and create our history through appreciation and realization of now.

> *My law it is in pleasure's paths to stray*
> *My creed to shun the theologic fray;*
> *I wedded Luck, and offered her a dower,*
> *She said, I want none, so thy heart be gay.*
> (Khayyam and Whinfield, 1980b, p. 40)

Khayyam's views on the question of life after death is complex. While his philosophical writing points to his belief in life after death, his poetry contradicts that view. As he puts it in the Rubaiyat: "Drink wine. This is life eternal. This is all that youth will give you. It is the season for wine, roses, and drunken friends. Be happy for this moment. This moment is your life" (Khayyam and Heron-Allen, 1898, p. 7).

While these positions may seem contradictory, one has to consider the hostility of the Islamic jurist to deviant views of life and death, taking a philosophical stance against the common reading of the scripture might have cost him his head; however, expressing the same concept in his poetry, he provides an alternative view of the life and death. Khayyam's philosophical stance can be attributed to his desire to establish a creative space to challenge common beliefs through art. Khayyam speaks of death as a cycle in life, the end of which is unknown, and thinking of it is pointless. What is available to us is the moment, with its unbounded possibilities; it is up to us to use it to break free from the predictable cycles of the cosmos. Khayyam clearly does not believe in a life after death nor resurrection.

> *My coming brought no profit to the sky,*
> *Nor does my going swell its majesty*
> *Coming and going put me to a stand,*
> *Ear never heard their wherefore nor their why.*
> (Khayyam and Whinfield, 1980b, p. 118)

LIFE AS INTEGRATION OF MOMENTS

Khayyam's interpretation of death is another stage in the universe's cycle, where our bodies are transformed and recycled into other matters.

Of mosque and prayer and fast preach not to me,
Rather go drink, were it on charity Yea, drink,
Khayyam, your dust will soon be made
A jug, or pitcher, or a cup, may be!
(Khayyam and Whinfield, 1980b, p. 276)

Denial of the afterlife was a supreme act of revolt against the established religious orthodoxy. However, it is essential to note that Khayyam's refusal of heaven and hell was not based on hedonistic tendencies but on escaping from the cycles of everydayness and mindless obedience. He compels us to flee from repetition and imitation since there are few possibilities and creativity in imitative life. Real and sustained happiness is to be extraordinary in every moment of life.

Khayyam tries to understand the world through observation and rationality while confessing to the inadequacy of our knowledge. Forming an understanding of the world is a never-ending intellectual journey, with euphoric moments of discovery followed by the sobriety of realizing the path ahead. Khayyam does not distract us from life with theories of the afterlife. He portraits the end for the powerful, the rich, and peasant alike; all will be turned into dust and clay, which might become a jar in the hands of a potter.

Who e'er returned of all that went before,
To tell of that long road they travel o'er?
Leave naught undone of what you have to do,
For when you go, you will return no more.
(Khayyam and Whinfield, 1980a, p. 174)

Declaring death as the end of life is not only brave but an act of rebellion; it is the necessary step for Khayyam's intellectual position on the significance of the moment. One would

LIFE AS INTEGRATION OF MOMENTS

not value something that has no end; such belief would entail inaction, leaving one's fate in the hands of powers that owe their continuity to their subjects' passivity. The idea of heaven and hell requires the belief that our lives extend beyond the grave, as no afterlife precludes the possibility of reward and punishment, which are the central tenet of Abrahamic religions. While believing in eternal reward in an imaginary afterlife might ease the oppressed's suffering, it does nothing for their everyday condition. If anything, it invites inaction and patience, exchanging revolt and defiance in the face of injustice with a promissory reward in a different world. Such an approach would amalgamate moments of life into a trail of suffering and obedience.

Such an approach would devalue the moment as it is not conducive to creativity and challenging the established rules sanctioned by the religious authorities, which aligns with governing powers prefer stability and advocate for conserving the status quo. Khayyam's position contrasts with religious leaders; he speaks of abandoning the idea of the afterlife, the imaginary world that no one has ever emerged from. He challenges us to ask why we should exchange the reality of here and now for a promissory fantasy?

> *My law it is in pleasure's paths to stray,*
> *My creed to shun the theologic fray*
> *I wedded Luck, and offered her a dower.*
> *She said, "I want none, so thy heart be gay."*
> (Khayyam and Whinfield, 1980a, p. 40)

> *They preach how sweet those Heaven angels will be,*
> *Hold fast this cash, and let that credit go.*
> *And shun the din of empty drums like me.*
> (Khayyam and Whinfield, 1980a, p. 40)

This is a radical and revolutionary position, in particular in the 11th century.

Notes

1. Khayyam explains the principles of algebra, for which he can be considered a precursor to Descartes in the invention of analytic geometry.
2. Translated by the author.
3. As predicted with precision in his work on calendar.

4

KHAYYAM, THE PEACE PROVOCATEUR

Khayyam's enthusiasm for tranquility and peace by gaining wisdom made him an ardent advocate for realism and avoiding unnecessary suffering. For Khayyam, peace was in avoiding past grief and future regrets. His philosophy was a quest to resurrect and maintain the flame of a rational framework of thought in the face of dogmatic reactions from religious jurists. On the other hand, he used poetry to expand the creative space for himself and for generations to come. At the same time, his scientific work extended rationality and brought math precision to our daily lives. The balance of his work provides a framework for looking at the world as it presents itself to us, contemplating the moment and enriching it with wisdom and joy of knowledge. Avoiding suffering and ignorance by seeking wisdom is the most significant gift of Khayyam to humanity and its struggle for peace. Khayyam focused his creativity and sharp mind against ignorance as to the source of evil and violence.

Khayyam invites us to experience life as an active participant rather than being an observer of its passage.

Facing uncertain death, what remains is to take control and direct our lives, enriching its every moment with the tranquility of knowledge and discovery. There is no greater sin than to blend in the indifferentiable masses, only governed by their habits, desires, and rituals.

Directing one's life means stepping in the individuation journey, realizing the value of its moment and embarking on unlocking the possibilities it could present. Individuation is an act of liberation; becoming a person means realizing the potential of life and opening our eyes to the world's beauty.

Khayyam compels us to break free from the prison of our repetitive lives. As a mathematician-astronomer, he knew well the predictable and deterministic cycles of the universe, using it in his poetry to warn us about the empty promises of an afterlife in a cyclical cosmos.

This act of rebellion against everydayness and uniformity is necessary to realize one's true potential. Khayyam's invitation to discover the potential of moments is vital for liberation from the banality of the masses.

It can be argued that one who realizes the value of time does not embark on destroying others' time. In Khayyam's worldview, avoiding unnecessary suffering is key in appreciating and realizing the moment. Considering suffering as one of the paradigms of violence, it is evident that he is an advocate of peace and tranquility.

Being attentive to the here and now is necessary for taking responsibility for one's condition of being. Improvement of life requires peaceful coexistence with others. Khayyamian world is not the world of Max Webber (Anter, 2020), where violence is a legitimate method for men's rule over men. As Hannah Arendt in *Men in Dark Times* writes:

> If it is the function of the public realm to throw light on the affairs of men by providing a space of appearances in which they can show in deed and word, for better and worse, who they are and what they can do, then darkness has come when this light is extinguished by "credibility gaps" and "invisible government, " by speech that does not disclose what is but sweeps it under the carpet, by exhortations, moral and otherwise, that under the pretext of upholding old truths, degrade all truth to meaningless triviality.
>
> (Arendt, 1970)

KHAYYAM, THE PEACE PROVOCATEUR

What is the parallel between the violence perpetrated on others during our time and Khayyam's teaching? Was he an advocate of having a good time or provocateur of peace by awakening and realizing one's place and time in the universe? What is common between Arendt's and Khayyam's argument is acting individualistically and following the path toward autonomy by avoiding predetermined play.

Khayyam's teachings emphasize liberation from the confines of dogmatic history as a key to happiness and fulfilling life's potentials. This act of freedom is a necessary step in the individuation process. In other words, becoming an individual is a prerequisite for taking responsibility for one's happiness. Khayyam's revolt against the tradition by creating an alternative way of thinking is the supreme act of resistance. His creativity and invitation to think differently is to explore and grab the life by its tail to embrace human senses to the fullest, remembering, forgetting, realizing, repeating, seeing, experiencing, or merely delving in the beauty of existence, bathing in the spring of life. It is to revitalize the personhood and experience the world and compose our own story of it. Such an approach would arguably result in a pluralist account of history and the world.

As Arendt once said, "the only way to teach people to think is to infect them with the perplexities that one is confronting" (Evans and Bernstein, 2017). Awakening the individuals and making them aware of the scarcity of their time in the world is the first step to restoring harmony in their lives. Peace is often considered harmony between individuals. Sustaining balance depends on a sense of well-being within individuals and oneness with the external environment.

That leads to the question of what it takes to create cooperation and harmony between individuals and groups.

Khayyam's answer to this question is to educate oneself about one time and place in this world. To see ourselves, not as automatons governed by imaginary rituals and habits but architects of our destiny, he advises us not to fall into the trap of impossible future, a mirage of never lands often sold by ideologues and charlatans. His advice on achieving happiness is to grab the world by its tail and be present to what makes us human, be aware of our potential of doing good and evil, and our authority in choosing our path in life. He rejects individuals' subordination to any other source; while we might not have control over how our life began, the rest is up to us. For Khayyam, happiness does not come by fulfilling ritualistic routines but by using our time creatively.

Being responsible for one's happiness is the first step in regaining an individual's authority over their destiny and restoring harmony in society.

It can be said that individuals in a Khayyamian society are aware of the temporal dimension of their life and know how to manage it. It is a society where individuals seek happiness through awareness, knowledge, and fulfillment of the potentials that every moment of life presents.

It is worth mentioning that Khayyam's view does not advocate hedonism and forgetfulness but awareness and being present. Understanding time requires sobriety, as drunkards lose their sense of time and place.

In such a society, individuals seek enrichment of their moments through acquiring knowledge and avoiding unnecessary suffering. In contrast, Khayyam advocates enjoying every moment of life; it should not be mistaken for promoting thoughtless hedonism.

Khayyam's opposition to the established belief of his era is evident in his poetry. His art contrasts with religious establishment teachings that discount the earthly life for a timeless afterlife. Khayyam's poetry speaks of love, experiencing life, and seeing the beauty in the world; in contrast, religion reduces humans to subjects that exist in a window of obedience.

Khayyam revolts against that mode of being, where the meaning of life is lost to shadows of unreachable future, where time stops and spontaneity and creativity of life is eschewed by angels, serving obedient automatons that have spent their cycles praying to an immutable God.

Khayyam's definition of life as the sum of its moment places the authority and responsibility of fulfilling it on individuals. It is a brave and revolutionary act, liberating us from the closed circuit of blindly churning the millstone of beliefs, in the realm of imaginary and inaccessible, to the world of direct experience, from being frightened of the shadows of the afterlife to touching, seeing, and tasting the skin of the lover, smelling the perfume, tasting the wine, seeing the best of the world as it presents itself to us, and avoiding suffering and hardship. It invites us to fulfill our lives with joy and happiness by realizing the potentials of its moment and follow rationality and the pursuit of knowledge.

Khayyam sees life and death as two sides of the same coin; this is not dissimilar from many other philosophers and intellectuals, Thomas Mann, Schopenhauer, and Nietzsche, to name a few, who thought about the question of life and death.

> *In a lone waste I saw a debauchee,*
> *He had no home, no faith, no heresy,*
> *No God, no truth, no law, no certitude*
> *Where in this world is man so bold as he?*
> (Khayyam and Whinfield, 1980a, p. 252)

The issues that Khayyam raised in his work are still pertinent today; we live in a world plagued by injustice. Modern technology has made our life more comfortable; however, it has failed to deliver happiness. Rationalism is still under attack by the orthodoxy of identity politics, tribalism, and relativism. Despite all its amenities, modern life has supplanted religion and ideology in subordinating humans and dictating cycles of their lives.

We live in a very different world from Omar Khayyam's while still facing the same existential questions about the meaning of life and death. Bookstores are filled with self-help books to help us have a more fulfilled life and to be more mindful of our existence. However, we cannot escape unhappiness without releasing ourselves from the millstone of everydayness that Khayyam warned us about nine centuries ago. To pursue happiness, we must first liberate our time from the harness that keeps it churning through an endless loop of suffering disguised as salvation.

Khayyam's writing tries to cajole and unchain us from the prison of habits, partially built by tradition and partly by our negligence of life, like a lazy bird pecking seed in its cage.

Khayyam tries to illustrate a framework of happiness. Applying it requires us to abandon habitual rituals and adopt a skeptical view of the world. To achieve happiness, one has to avoid unnecessary suffering, which involves coexistence and empathy.

As Thomas Mann (1937) has argued, "Man is nature's fall from grace, only it is not a fall, but just as positively an elevation as conscience is higher than innocence." He writes That original sin "is the deep feeling of man as a spiritual being for his natural infirmities and limitations, above which he raises himself through spirit" (Mann, 1942).

In Khayyam's worldview, rising and awareness are through realizing the bounded and limited existence in the world. His revolt against the ritualistic and repetitive way of life is still relevant today. The authority for routines and rituals has shifted from religious leaders to global corporations and political establishments.

In the *The Coming Victory of Democracy*, Mann argued for the democracy:

> [Democracy] is a "spiritual and moral possession." It is not just rules; it is a way of life. It encourages everybody to make the best of their capacities—holds that we have a moral responsibility to do so. It encourages the artist to seek beauty, the neighbor to seek community, the psychologist to seek perception, the scientist to seek truth.
> (Brooks, 2017)

The moral and spiritual dimension of democracy is the connecting rod of individual humanism of Khayyam; it is informed by science and inspired by art.

It is important to note that Khayyam's attention to the moment does not imply satisfying our short-lived senses and instincts. His attention to aesthetics and desire to achieve happiness is a struggle to give meaning to our existence. It is a form of resistance against the established forces that subjugate humanity to power structures by destroying its creative space and sovereignty over time.

Khayyam's poetry is a call to action; being present and aware of the moment does not mean having a short horizon; on the contrary, it means unleashing creativity and bringing the possibilities of the future and the heritage of the past to the present. Khayyam was aware of his mortality; if he believed in a meaningless world, he would not leave us such valuable work of science and art. He points to his struggle of unlocking this world's secrets and his awe at how much of it is inaccessible and unknown.

> *Never was my hearth deprived of science*
> *Delved I did into many mysterious*
> *From Dawn to dusk, for Seventy two years I seek*
> *Discovered at last, I know naught.*[1]
>
> (Foroughi, 1976)

It is clear that Khayyam believes in the incompleteness of human knowledge; however, he does not cede authority over his time to the guardians of the established belief.

Studying his poetry and science relieves a person from customary practices, as habits factorize the moments, turn them into undifferentiated cycles, and numb creativity.

This numbness and indifference are the sources of evil and destructive to creativity. Khayyam invites us to use the power of intellect to comprehend our place in this world and avoid chasing pointless pursuits.

> *The stars, who dwell on heaven's exalted stage,*
> *Baffle the wise diviners of our age*
> *Take heed, hold fast the rope of mother wit.*
> *These augurs all distrust their own presage.*
>
> (Khayyam and Whinfield, 1980a, p. 144)

This numbness and indifference is the source of evil and destructive to creativity. No one knows if Khayyam had access to Seneca's writings, but both seem to agree when it comes to realizing the value of our time:

> There is no reason for you to think that any man has lived long because he has grey hairs or wrinkles; he has not lived long—he has existed long. For what if you should think that that man had had a long voyage who had been caught by a fierce storm as soon as he left the harbor, and, swept hither and thither by a succession of winds that raged from different quarters, had been driven in a circle around the same course? Not much voyaging did he have, but much tossing about.
> (Seneca, 2005)

Or about the futility of living for the future:

> The greatest obstacle to living is expectancy, which hangs upon tomorrow and loses today. . . . The whole future lies in uncertainty: live immediately.
> (Khayyam and Whinfield, 1980a, p. 74)

Living immediately and purposefully is the core message in Seneca's essay and the focus of Khayyam's poetry.

Becoming attentive to what matters requires avoiding distraction. Distraction is a departure from being present and realizing its potentials; it is the evil that destroys possibilities. Distraction blocks joy; it prevents us from employing our rationality and expanding our creative space. Distraction from the immediacy of life and its experience is the most destructive act that impedes freedom and is an essential tool for tyrants to subjugate their subjects.

A distracted populace is easy to rule and dominate; they conform and follow sheepishly as long as their attention span is managed and controlled by the output of propaganda machinery; their focus is obscured by the amazement of the shameless spectacle, filled with grotesque and rudeness.

As Davis Foster Wallace puts it:

> To me, at least in retrospect, the really interesting question is why dullness proves to be such a powerful impediment to attention. Why we recoil from the dull. Maybe it's because dullness is intrinsically painful; maybe that's where phrases like "deadly dull" or "excruciatingly dull" come from. But there might be more to it. Maybe dullness is associated with psychic pain because something that's dull or opaque fails to provide enough stimulation to distract people from some other, deeper type of pain that is always there, if only in an ambient, low-level way, and which most of us spend nearly all our time and energy trying to distract ourselves from feeling, or at least from feeling directly or with our full attention. Admittedly, the whole thing's pretty confusing, and hard to talk about abstractly . . . but surely something must lie behind not just Muzak in dull or tedious places any more but now also actual TV in waiting rooms, supermarkets' checkouts, airport gates, SUVs' backseats. Walkman, iPods, BlackBerries, cell phones that attach to your head. This terror of silence with nothing diverting to do. I can't think anyone really believes that today's so-called "information society" is just about information. Everyone knows it's about something else, way down.
> (Wallace, 2014)

Khayyam advocates for awareness and attention which by no means is hedonistic, as attentiveness reveals the painful truth about our existence and the human condition. As Nietzsche said,

> We labour at our daily work more ardently and thoughtlessly than is necessary to sustain our life because it is even more necessary not to have leisure to stop and think. haste is universal because everyone is in flight from himself.
> (Swanton, 2015)

Life is an integration of its attentive moments sans its distracted moments. Distraction might be a way to forget our existence's dullness; it is not easy to accept the meaninglessness of ordinary life; being extraordinary requires engagement with the world and be prepared for its peril and excitement.

Khayyam poetry is a way for us to learn about taking control of our lives by becoming actors rather than spectators. In Khayyam's worldview, life and its experience are verifiable and at hand. At the same time, the afterlife and all its promises and fears are, at best, hypothetical and subject to speculation and doubt.

This leads to the realization of the moment's potency, as freedom can only be achieved through emancipation from the constraints of the past and unknowns of the future.

As we expand the possibilities of the moment, it reveals itself to us as a mode of being, away from everydayness and distraction, with an intense focus on what is available and is at hand. It is the path to revitalizing creativity and liberating the temporal dimension from the uniformity of herds. It is the prerequisite to becoming an individual. It can be argued that the individuation process depends on one's ability to assert their will on their time.

Khayyam's poetry is evidence for his firm belief in life as being an integration of its moment; he denies the afterlife in numerous quartets,

> *"How Sweet is mortal Sovranty!"-think some;*
> *Others-"How blest the Paradise to come!"*
> *Ah, take the Cash in hand and waive the Rest;*
> *Oh, the brave Music of a distant Drum!*
>
> (FitzGerald, 1997, p. 11)

Temporizing is the act of resistance to change, as change can be disruptive to the cycle of life; it is often easier to attribute life's misery to one's fate than taking responsibility for it.

Avoiding change impedes the will and deprives life of possibilities and choices. Being present is discovering life opportunities to transition to a better state of being and elevate the human condition. Procrastination is irrational as it betrays the possibility of transformation by a false promise of action in the future; it will supplant autonomy, surrendering oneself to the opaque power, be it the authoritarian establishment, tradition, or merely the lifestyle one has blindly accepted.

As Emmanuel Kant puts it:

> Enlightenment is man's release from his self-incurred tutelage. Tutelage is man's inability to make use of his understanding without direction from another.
>
> Self-incurred is this tutelage when its cause lies not in lack of reason but in lack of resolution and courage to use it without direction from another.
> (Gascoigne, 2013)
>
> Have courage to use your own reason!' that's the motto of enlightenment.
> (Kant, 1784, p. 462)

It can be argued that Khayyam's emphasis on valuing life's precious moments cannot be realized without having the freedom to choose. The choice is between inaction, being a passenger of the history, and participating and experiencing history. There is a stark contrast between passivity and enablement and self-determinism.

It is essential to put that in historical context, as two prevalent forces of his era, Sufism and religious orthodoxy, both emphasize different forms of fatalism and passivity.[2]

> Islamic mysticism has its roots in the primordial covenant relationship described in Qur'ān 7: 172. The earliest phase of Sufism, the ascetical tradition, focuses on the presence of evil within man and the world. The later development of the science of opposites by ecstatic mystics results in an elitist ethical system whose ground is the mystical relationship, not the sharī'ah. The seeds of this

development can be found in the classical Ash'arite synthesis. Finally, Ibn Arabī's relentlessly deterministic elaboration of waḥdat al-wujūd, the unity of Being, reduces man's individual moral choice to an illusion, except insofar as man realizes himself to be one with God.

(Awn, 1983)

In other words, living in passivity and abstaining from assessing one's will over time is living without awareness. Life without awareness is not much different than a state of unconsciousness; unaware and passive beings are observers and passengers of time, unable to realize their potentials and change their course. Such existence is not much different from Zombie-like creatures, unconscious about the time, only responding to immediate stimuli. Being present in time and space is a prerequisite to asserting free will and gaining autonomy; being conscious means being present in life moments.

Moments cannot be captured, but they ought to be experienced; much like snowflakes, it melts upon touch, leaving an impression of its journey, from the sea, over the mountains, through the cloud, and finally falling back on the earth, quenching the thirst of the parched land to tend to the bulb of Poppy and to furnish the desert red in the spring.

Khayyam sees life as an end in itself; this is a view shared by philosopher Emmanuel Kant; according to Kant, a rational person should be treated as an end in themselves. Humanity is valuable in itself.

That would entail that humanity does not derive its value from something else. There is inherent value in our existence as humans.

> Act in such a way that you always treat humanity, whether in your own person or in the person of any other, never merely as a means but still at the same time as an end.
>
> (Hill, 1980)

The traits of Khayyam's worldview can be found among many contemporary philosophers and freethinkers worldwide;

for instance, the similarities between Khayyam's take on the importance of life, as experienced in the moment, with Aurobindo concept of terrestrial life is noteworthy;

> Aurobindo held that terrestrial life itself, in its higher evolutionary stages, is the real goal of creation. He believed that the basic principles of matter, life, and mind would be succeeded through terrestrial evolution by the principle of supermind as an intermediate power between the two spheres of the infinite and the finite. Such a future consciousness would help to create a joyful life in keeping with the highest goal of creation, expressing values such as love, harmony, unity and knowledge and successfully overcoming the age-old resistance of dark forces against efforts to manifest the divine on earth.
> (Britannica, 2021)

Focus on terrestrial life as a path to create joyful life is strikingly Khayyamian. Focus on individual and life as an end in itself and not as a means to achieve eternal salvation predates the modern notion of individuality by several centuries.

Being in time is being with others; it requires becoming active. Activation is a de-zombification process, rather than responding to stimuli from their environment or habits. Passivity is to be the subject of rituals of life and religion. Passivity enslaves people to their habits and traditions. Surprisingly, notion of individuality has done little to emancipate humans from their immaturity. Passivity and determinism effectively separate us from our creativity and demote a person from responsibility for their happiness.

Responsibility for one's happiness is the first step in the individuation process and questioning and challenging things detrimental to personal happiness.

Being responsible for one's happiness is the path to pacifism and nonviolence. It is noteworthy to emphasize violence role in the destruction of fundamental elements of happiness, namely the social fabric and creativity, according to the World Health organization:

> Violence is a universal scourge that tears at the fabric of communities and threatens the life, health and happiness of us all. Each year, more than 1.6 million people worldwide lose their lives to violence. For everyone who dies as a result of violence, many more are injured and suffer from a range of physical, sexual, reproductive and mental health problems. Violence is among the leading causes of death for people aged 15–44 years worldwide, accounting for about 14% of deaths among males and 7% of deaths among females.
> (World Health Organization, 1999)

Therefore, it is evident that the path to happiness does not go through the valley of violence; in the same token, it can be argued that happiness is not a product of luck, as it is a state of mind that requires awareness and conscious choices. While luck may bring pleasant surprise, it is not an assured path to achieve happiness. According to Aristotle, "Happiness depends on ourselves" (Hongladarom and Joaquin, 2021). In Aristotle's view, happiness is achieved by living a life of "virtuous activity in accordance with reason"—that leads to the perfection of human nature and the enrichment of human life (Sherman, 1999). Taking such a path to happiness compels us to make choices, some of which might not be easy. Khayyam view on happiness is not dissimilar,

> *I cannot hide the Sun for dust I raise!*
> *And cannot speak the secrets of the days.*
> *The pearl, which I have brought from wisdom deep,*
> *If strung may lose the splendour of its ray!*
> (Tirtha and Khayyam, 1941, p. 297)

> *The good and evil with man's nature blent,*
> *The weal and woe that heaven's decrees have sent,*

Impute them not to motions of the skies,
Skies than thyself ten times more impotent.
(Khayyam and Whinfield, 1980a, p. 66)

On the one hand, free will and being present to own's condition of life and choices are the prerequisite of happiness; on the other hand, passivity is the path to serfdom and self-induced immaturity. As Emanuel Kant (1999) puts it in his famous essay, "Answering the Question: What Is Enlightenment?" (German: Beantwortung der Frage: Was ist Aufklärung?): "Enlightenment is man's emergence from his self-incurred immaturity (Unmündigkeit)." Kant argues that the lack of courage to apply own reasons and intellect, free from a directive from others, be it the servants of God or other humans, is the cause of immaturity and being minor. Kant's motto of the Enlightenment—Dare to be wise! is the acknowledgment of the perils and opportunities of autonomy in reasoning.

Khayyam's scientific approach, as well as his poetry, points to a skeptical scientist-artists; his skepticism was in contrast with the belief system promoted by the religious and political establishment of the era. According to Sadeq Hedayat, Khayyam was an ardent atheist:

> while Khayyam believes in the transmutation and transformation of the human body, he does not believe in a separate soul; if we are lucky, our bodily particles would be used in the making of a jug of wine.
> (Katouzian, 1991)

As defined by the Encyclopedia Britannica, skepticism is

> the attitude of doubting knowledge claims set forth in various areas. Skeptics have challenged the adequacy or reliability of these claims by asking what principles they are based upon or what they actually establish. They have questioned whether some such claims really are, as alleged, indubitable or necessarily true, and

they have challenged the purported rational grounds of accepted assumptions.

(Popkin, 2020)

As an intellectual, he was deeply committed to understanding the universe; however, setting up a rational framework for intellectual interrogation of values and beliefs, religious conviction and certitude posed a problem.

> Religion has proved incapable of surmounting his inherent fears; thus, Khayyam finds himself alone and insecure in a universe about which his knowledge is nil.
> (Katouzian, 1991)

Omar was hated and dreaded by the Sufis, whose practice he ridiculed and whose faith amounts to little more than his own, when stripped of the Mysticism and formal recognition of Islamism under which Omar would not hide.

(Khayyam et al., 1997, p. 6)

The importance of Khayyam's skepticism becomes apparent when considering the dominant ideologies of his era: Sufism and Islamic orthodoxy. Both ideologies were at odds with Khayyam's humanistic rationalism, which questioned their path to certitude; after all, Khayyam acknowledged the limit of human knowledge and saw rationality and art as the only path to happiness.

> *Some look for truth in creeds, and forms, and rules*
> *Some grope for doubts or dogmas in the schools*
> *But from behind the veil a voice proclaims,*
> *"Your road lies neither here nor there, fools."*
> (Khayyam and Whinfield, 1980a, p. 66)

It is often quoted that Attar, who is considered the grand expert on Sufism, thought of Khayyam as a freethinking rationalist who chooses the path of reason over revelation (Boyle, 1969; Browne, 1959).

Like any other freethinking scientist and artist, he was skeptical, questioning our existence, the origin of this world, and its destiny. What makes him exceptional is the balance between his philosophy, art, and science; he was the towering figure in history who managed to stand at the intersection of philosophy, art, and science.

Khayyam's Rubaiyat is an act of rebellion against the Zeitgeist of his era; he is not there to create another dogmatic ideology; his project is intellectual and educative, to pursue knowledge and expand creative space. Appreciation of the moments means engaging with the world. The act of abandoning the afterlife means focusing on this world as the only source and destination and alerting us to our time's scarcity and value. As violence is the biggest threat to time, it can be argued that abandoning the afterlife and focusing on there and now has the potential to reduce the tendency for violence.

> *In a lone waste I saw a debauchee,*
> *He had no religion, no Islam, no worldliness, no heresy,*
> *No God, no truth, no sharia, no certitude*
> *Where in this world is man so bold as he?*
> (Whinfiled, p. 252, modified by the author)

The universal communicability of aesthetics (Kalar, 2006) is the glue that binds the individuals, as judging spectators, in society. Valuing and comprehending beauty and work of art requires thinking; therefore, the artwork is not merely an object that stimulates senses but creates a possibility space that enriches the moment as it is interacted with. In other words, art has temporal possibilities, expanding spectators' space and creativity as they interact with it. Hannah Arendt called the artwork "thought things," "hybrids of spirit and material object which express ideas that elude easy discursive formulation. This concept draws upon the Kantian theme of ideas that cannot be directly experienced." (Sjöholm, 2015, p. 219).

KHAYYAM, THE PEACE PROVOCATEUR

As Hannah Arendt wrote in *The Crisis in Culture*,

> From the viewpoint of their durability, artworks are superior to all things; since they stay longer in the world than anything else, they are the only things without function in the life process of society; strictly speaking, they are fabricated not for men, but for the world which is meant to outlast the life-span of mortals, the coming and going of generations.
>
> (Arendt and Kohn, 2006)

The transformative impact of thinking induced by art expands the creative space and challenges the status quo. Art is everlasting, yet mutable as it gains new meaning with time, as fine wine improves with the passage of time. Art is the engine of innovation and the source of mutation and change. Thorough art imagining the impossible is permissible, and reconciling the incompatibles becomes probable. Work of Art, be it a fine bottle of wine or masterfully composed music, has the creative potential beyond what is imagined by its creators, as the individual experience of interaction with artwork is both unique and communal. It is communal so that it is shared by the society (Ginsborg, 2005) and unique in a way that expands the creative space of the person interacting with it. In other words, art, if comprehended, has an activating effect on its spectators. In Khayyam's poetry, being and living with aesthetic aspects of life is considered paramount, where spectatorship of beauty is an art. To put it differently, being in the moment is an act of conscious interaction with aesthetic elements of life.

Unlike ideology and religion, art does not demand obedience but contemplation and collaboration. Work of art is the combination of the cultural pattern of its era. Significant art gains information and potency over time; for example, Picasso's Guernica, as an anti-war protest masterpiece, continues to be a source of inspiration for many generations of artists to express resistance by appealing to aesthetic senses.

Art inspires and activates its recipients; it carries the spirit of its era through time, engaging its spectators. Art has the potency to convert spectators into active participants, kindling their imagination and creativity so they can reach out and grasp the experience of the artwork through its journey, much like drinking an aged fine bottle of wine, not only hearing as it recites its story but becoming a cast in the play.

> *Khayyam! if drunk with wine, rejoice*
> *If in company of beauty, rejoice*
> *Since none will last, Suppose you were no more,*
> *Rejoice then that you are.*[3]

Art not only brings heaven down to the earth but emancipates the heavenly features from immutability to enrich and transform the world. It is the potency of art, to create and shift borders of thought, that makes it the subject of ire from the guardian of the tradition and religious orthodoxy.

A great work of art captures the essence and spirit of its era; in other words, it is the reflection of Zeitgeist.

> Hegel believed that art reflected, by its very nature, the culture of the time in which it is created. Culture and art are inextricable because an individual artist is a product of his or her time and therefore brings that culture to any given work of art.
>
> (Hendrix, 2005)

It is noteworthy that while Rubaiyat is the evidence of a poet with a humanistic yet spiritual, the transcendence power of art and Khayyam's perspective on life makes the Rubaiyat spiritual (Diffey, 1994), as Pablo Picasso said, "Art washes away from the soul the dust of everyday life" (Klein, 2012).

> *Khayyam! rejoice that wine you still can pour,*
> *And still the charms of tulip cheeks adore;*

> *You'll soon not be, rejoice then that you are,*
> *Think how 'twould be in case you were no more!*
>
> (Khayyam and Whinfield, 1980a, p. 190)

Making peace is a creative act; like any other form of creativity, it requires taming violence and supplanting domination with empathy and understanding. Through rebinding with this world and its beauties, one can create an account of its collective consciousness. Understanding art is to understand our existence; it is an educative process that elevates the taste and places the human experience in a profound and accurate perspective.

Through poetry, Khayyam shows us the path to reconcile opposing views peacefully, standing at the cross section of science, philosophy, and art. He deliberately challenges his philosophical position in his art. It can be argued that sustainable peace requires the transformation of Zeitgeist.

Avoiding suffering and pursuing happiness requires valuing every moment of life and taking responsibility for one's condition. Khayyamian world loathes violence, as it is the biggest threat to peace, harmony, and everything that makes sustained happiness and joy possible. Khayyam does not provide a prescription on putting an end to human suffering; however, he reminds us that our essence is the source of good and evil in the world. Therefore, the responsibility of taming the violence and ensuring peace is on us, not God.

> *The good and evil with man's nature blent,*
> *The weal and woe that heaven's decrees have sent,*
> *Impute them not to motions of the skies,*
> *Skies than thyself ten times more impotent.*
>
> (Khayyam and Whinfield, 1980a, p. 66)

Becoming aware of one's potential to do good and evil is the first and necessary step to taking responsibility for a peaceful world. It is noteworthy to remind that peace is not absent of violence, but it is the state of happiness, joy, and enlightenment in the Khayyamian frame of mind.

KHAYYAM, THE PEACE PROVOCATEUR

Don't fret in vain but live in peace and glee,
Be ever just though folk unjust would be;
This world at last, you know, will vanish, hence
Shake off thy body, live for ever free.
(Tirtha and Khayyam, 1941, p. 96)

As the wheel of the world runs, we feel the passage of time and its domination, as every aspect of life and culture is synchronized and measured by time. Passage of time and years can be calculated mathematically, as Khayyam masterfully showed us by devising his era's most precise calendar; however, time is also a mystery. It is natural to conclude that for Khayyam, time was as compelling as the origins of the cosmos and the nature of our existence.

The question is how changing our attitude toward time could bring peace to this world. Can the Khayyamian way of life reduce violence and allow peace to hold? Reading Khayyam's poetry gives an impression that he viewed time as discrete moments, which should be valued and enriched by seeking happiness and joy. However, to avoid boredom and repetitiveness, one needs to live creatively. The art of life is to enrich every moment creatively. It can be said that meaningful life is the integration of its creative moments, where possibilities emerge from questioning and challenging established beliefs, be it self-imposed or governed by social or religious hierarchy and power structure.

Khayyam shows the path through his art; he lived in a dangerous era, when being a freethinker placed one in great peril. He had a choice, to synchronize his work and way of life with the established narrative and live in peace, or resist and create a new path and risk his life. Khayyam chooses to think dangerously, transcending the imposed barriers erected by the religious orthodoxies. By risking his safety, Khayyam not only created a new path but shows us how to overcome a suffocating dogmatism. Art was his secret weapon against the oppressive ideology of the time. In his *Rubā'iyyāt*, he questions not only the core of the Zeitgeist but his philosophical position.

KHAYYAM, THE PEACE PROVOCATEUR

Khayyam's mode of resistance is essential in maintaining and expanding the creative space, which is a fundamental enabler of peace.

Peace cannot be sustained without creativity, as social time emerges from creative moments experienced individually and socially. A society without creativity is trapped in passivity and repetitive cycle of ritual spectacles and is vulnerable to authoritarian rule.

> *My critics call me a philosopher,*
> *But God knows full well they greatly err;*
> *I know not even what I am, much less*
> *Why on this earth I am a sojourner.*
>
> (Khayyam and Whinfield, 1980a, p. 234)

Skepticism is a central theme of the Khayyamian mode of being; while some have deciphered it as bewilderment and confusion, it is indeed the sign of a rational scholar understanding the boundaries of the knowledge and what lies beyond it.

> *In the loop we come and go,*
> *with no beginning nor an end*
> *No one knows the its truth*
> *where we come from, where we go.*[4]

Khayyam skepticism should not be mistaken with the state of confusion about our existence and the origin of this world. Khayyam's rational thinking is in clear contrast with the dominant myth-making mode of thinking of his era. The evident skepticism (Vogt, 2018, p. 97) in *Rubāʿiyyāt* points to Pyrrhonism, not showing signs of bewilderment but suspending judgment in the face of difficult questions and inaccessible truth.

> *I thought my heart had caught His lovely glow,*
> *I thought His secrets were as what I trow,*
> *But now with wisdom's eyes I scan myself*
> *And see that know I naught for aught I know.*
>
> (Tirtha and Khayyam, 1941, p. 245)

KHAYYAM, THE PEACE PROVOCATEUR

Khayyam's skeptical view of the world, in particular acknowledging the incompleteness of knowledge, contrasted with the established orthodoxy's certitude, which was intolerant to any intellectual position that cast doubt on its dogmas. Suspension of judgment is an act of liberation of the mind from the trap of dogmatic ideology and repetitive cycles of habits and rituals.

A consistent element in Khayyam's philosophical, scientific, and artistic work is his skeptical and investigative approach dealing with both mysteries and established beliefs of his era. By suspending his belief and showing the courage to bring into question the tenet of religious orthodoxy, in particular the afterlife, not only did he manage to disrupt the boundaries of the established beliefs, thus expanding the creative space, but he challenged the political system that tried to dominate every aspect of human existence.

Freethinking and skepticism in the face of certitude and dogmatism are acts of resistance and the foundation of tolerance. Through poetry and the power of art, Khayyam opened a path between the dominant forces of his time: Islamic orthodoxy and Sufism. Khayyamian way of life is founded on rationality, critical thinking, and valuing the potency of the aware moments.

It is an individuate process, where liberation from the homogeneity of herd mentality is the required step to become aware of one's place and time in the world, and to be present to life and its unrepeatable moments and possibilities.

Moments emerge from interaction with the creative space; meaningful moments are those that create new possibilities. Valuing the moments requires making choices about what and who we interact with. Awareness and becoming an active partner in the interaction space are necessary to have meaningful moments and ensure happiness.

On the other hand, awareness requires questioning and critical thinking, which are the tenant of rationality and creativity. The creative moments that have emerged from the intentional choice of interaction space and time have the potential to lead to happiness and joy. Being aware and applying free will and critical thinking is essential in the proper choice of the interaction[5] partner.

> *Assume, eludes you the secrets of the universe*
> *And Remote is the wise technique*
> *Rise and raise a paradise from wine and green*
> *As in heaven, you may arrive or not.*[6]
>
> (Foroughi, 1976)

The liberating potency of the Khayyamian worldview is essential in achieving inner peace. Seeing the world, as it presents itself to us, with all its mysteries and accepting the transient nature of our existence is the path to awakening and taking control of precious moments of life.

Liberation from dogma is the first step in disrupting the repetitive, mythical, and manipulating narrative fueling the engine of religious tyranny.

> *Some look for truth in creeds, and forms, and rules*
> *Some grope for doubts or dogmas in the schools*
> *Suddenly a voice proclaims,*
> *"The path lies neither here nor there, you fools.*
>
> (Khayyam and Whinfield, 1980a, p. 52, modified by the author)

Finding inner peace is a personal journey and in extension, a required step in establishing peace in society; as Confucius taught,

> To put the world in order, we must first put the nation in order; to put the nation in order, we must put the family in order; to put the family in order, we must cultivate our personal life; and to cultivate our personal life, we must first set our hearts right.
>
> (Moon, 2012)

It can be argued that the Khayyamian project's aim is the intellectual emancipation of humans from the grip of stultifying guardians and masters of tradition of religion.

The act of liberation from the self-stultifying masters (Ranciere, 1991, p. 99) allows the individuals to emerge from their nonage, expand their creative space, and step into enlightenment. As Emanuel Kant puts it:

> Enlightenment is man's emergence from his self-imposed nonage. Nonage is the inability to use one's understanding without another's guidance. This nonage is self-imposed if its cause lies not in lack of understanding but in indecision and lack of courage to use one's mind without another's guidance. Dare to know! (Sapere aude.). Have the courage to use your own understanding.
> (Kant and Smith, 2020)

While centuries apart, there are striking similarities in Kant and Khayyam's approach to the role of freethinking and independent decision-making.

> *For "Is" and "Is-not" though with Rule and Line,*
> *And "Up-and-down" without, I could define,*
> *I yet in all I only cared to know,*
> *Was never deep in anything but—Wine.*
> (FitzGerald, 1997, p 176)

> *Am I a wine-bibber? What if I am?*
> *Zoroastrians, or infidel? Suppose I am?*
> *Each sect envision me, what I am not,*
> *I am my own, and, what I am, I am.*
> (Khayyam and Whinfield, 1980b, p. 225)

While Khayyam's poetry sometimes has been interpreted as hedonistic, he is not an advocate for an unrestrained pursuit of pleasure; on the contrary, he is intensely focused on the power of life as the engine that moves us toward the aesthetic aspect of life. Khayyam does not provide an ideology; he shows us how to comprehend the world as it presents itself to us, with all its mysteries and complexities, and avoid reducing its perplexing puzzles into simplistic concepts. Khayyam recognizes the fallibility of human knowledge and invites us to focus on making the most out of our time on the earth instead of spending life chasing myths.

> *Assume, eludes you the secrets of the universe*
> *And Remote is the wise technique*
> *Rise and raise a paradise from wine and green*
> *As in heaven, you may arrive or not.*[7]

(Foroughi, 1976)

Bringing heaven down to the earth is a radical move, making God accessible to humans and reachable by reason. Khayyam dared to question God's wisdom for suffering and evil in this world; he asked the hard question, why punish humans for the act that they cannot be deemed responsible for?

> *As burden me with the destiny, without me*
> *Why calling to account me*
> *Yesterday, today, alike, without me*
> *Tomorrow, how to judge me.*[8]

Fatalism is irreconcilable with divine judgment and moral responsibility. How humans could be responsible for their deeds if they are predestined in this world. Khayyam's rational mind rejects the idea of the predestined world.

> *Source of joy and sorrow, We*
> *Reserve of justice, origin of tyranny, We*
> *Vile and pleasant, perfect and inferior, We*
> *Rusted mirror, Cup of Jamshid, We.*[9]

While Khayyam does not reject the creator's idea for this world, his poetry shows his belief in free will. Khayyamian way of life is spiritual yet rational. At the same time, it recognizes suffering and death as realities; it rejects the idea that humans are condemned to suffer and toil for a reason other than their actions. It reconnects the individuals with the world and themselves, removing the veil and allowing them to feel the wind, smell the flowers, and taste the wine. It is the act of breaking the yoke of guilt that is placed on our back for the sin of seeking beauty. The first step in the individuation process is reconnecting with the self as the source of evil and good. Rather than avoiding the question of evil, the Khayyamian worldview sees it as a complementary force, that along with good, interacts within a greater whole. As the Greek philosopher Heraclitus (2017) said, "Good and evil are one."

It can be argued that the Khayyamian way of life is a path to individuation, as elaborated in the 20th century by Carl Jung in *Two Essays on Analytical Psychology*:

> Individuation means becoming an "in-dividual," and, in so far as "individuality" embraces our innermost, last, and incomparable uniqueness, it also implies becoming one's self. We could therefore translate individuation as "coming to selfhood" or "self-realization."
> (Jung, 1966)

The relationship between peace and a strong sense of individuality is noteworthy; individuality and freethinking encourage tolerance in society. To satisfy the sense of belonging, fellowship, family, or companionship, individuals have to develop their ability to cooperate and tolerate other individuals. The homogeneity promoted by religious orthodoxy and some ideologies is a barrier for the individuation process as they frown upon pluralism, deviance, skepticism, and being different. It is important to note a clear distinction between individuality and individualism, as explained by Sacvan Bercovitch (Bercovitch, 2014) in his book, *The Rites of Assent*, "Emerson, Individualism, and Liberal Dissent." Developing based on Emerson's notions of individuality and individualism, he provides a distinction between "individualism" and "individuality." He argues that "individualism" views life as competitive while "individuality" promotes the sense of community through self-awareness and self-development (Emerson et al., 1971).

It can be argued that the Khayyamian worldview is also an individualistic project, whereby self-development is achieved by living creatively, achieving diversity yet preserving cohesion. Its essence is rebellious and anti-structure, ridiculing dogma and established orthodoxies rather than promoting a creative way of life.

In the Khayyamian worldview, the individual bears the responsibility for the human condition and their destiny. It is this transfer from the divine to the individual that is the foundation of his freethinking.

Khayyamian individual is liberated and independent; they refuse to accept inherited and imported orthodoxies and are empowered with a sense of responsibility for their happiness.

On the other side is the uninformed and passive masses, which allow the established orthodoxies' rituals to dictate their destiny. The institutionalized tradition of religion and ideologies creates megastructures that are intolerant to dissent and creativity. They impose uniformity and homogeneity, often with brutal force.

Imposing a culture of uniformity and suppressing dissent is a recipe for violence and threatens peace.

It is essential to note the difference between unity and uniformity; the latter frowns upon differences while the former recognizes differences.

As Pope Francis, in a meeting with Myanmar religious leaders, puts it, "United does not mean the same; unity is not uniformity, even within the same confession," and also said "Each one has its values, its riches, and also its deficiencies." He added that in life, as in music, harmony comes from uniting differences, not eliminating them (Brockhaus, 2018).

Peace is an art and act of creativity; it unites the differences while preserving their uniqueness, transforming perpetrators into performers in an ensemble of harmony, where rage is transformed into creativity, and fear gives way to cooperation.

For Khayyam, living peacefully is the path to achieving joy and happiness. His way of life is essentially a personal project that depends on the awareness of the world and life's transient and impermanent nature.

Since no one can assure thee of the morrow,
Rejoice thy heart to-day, and banish sorrow
With moon bright wine, fair moon, for heaven's moon
Will look for us in vain on many a morrow.
                              (Khayyam and Whinfield, 1980b, p. 6)

Defining life as the integration of its moments is a fundamental element of the Khayyamian worldview and the prerequisite to achieving a meaningful existence. The significance of the moment, as a discrete variable of time, is in its potential in the creative space-time, where beauty can be experienced and curated.

Here with a Loaf of Bread beneath the Bough,
A Flask of Wine, a Book of Verse—and Thou
Beside me singing in the Wilderness—
And Wilderness is Paradise enow.
                              (Khayyam et al., 1997)

The Khayyamian way of life creates peace in the world by awakening the masses and turning them into individuals, sharpening their senses to the beauties of this world and making them aware of their impermanency in the cosmos. It brings heaven and hell down to the earth, liberating humans from the fear of eternal condemnation or the illusion of salvation. The only salvation needed is from the dogmatic orthodoxies of established power that ruin the moments of life on this earth with the false promise of an afterlife in an imaginary heaven

They preach how sweet those Heaven angels will be,
But I say wine is sweeter—taste and see
Hold fast this cash, and let that credit go.
And shun the din of empty drums like me.
                              (Khayyam and Whinfield, 1980b, p. 40)

It is essential to point out the distinction between harmony and peace. Peace maintains balance and a framework for creative forces to disrupt the status quo while preserving individual rights to freedom and liberty. Freethinking and creativity are essential elements of an innovative and artistic way of life, which inevitably disrupts existing norms and tradition. Peace is the inclusive framework that allows the disruptive forces of art and creativity to transform social norms. While harmony promotes coexistence, it should not be used to preserve the status quo and encourage segregation.

Like Nietzsche, Khayyam sees life as an aesthetic experience; being with beauty is an artistic act. The expansion of creative space allows innovation and art to flourish and transform the space-time, making art and beauty possible and sustainable. In other words, art and creativity have a symbiotic relationship; art enrichment of the moment enables creativity, which creates the condition for appreciation and interaction with art. Nietzsche's characterization of his view of the world as "the world as a work of art that gives birth to itself" can be reconciled with the Khayyamian perspective. In comparison, Nietzsche sees art as a way to escape pessimism from realizing the failure of our cognitive power to lead us to the truth (Lanier, 2017). In contrast, Khayyam considers the aesthetic experience not an escape but the only moment worth living.

> *Assume, eludes you the secrets of the universe*
> *And Remote is the wise technique*
> *Rise and raise a paradise from wine and green*
> *As in heaven, you may arrive or not.*[10]

What leads both Khayyam and Nietzsche to art and beauty is the fallibility of our knowledge and cognitive power to solve world mysteries. Khayyamian aesthetic worldview leads to creativity and beauty; his plea to create heaven on the earth, from earthly material, is a call to creativity and invention.

> *Since naught we hold in hand of ought but air,*
> *Since ought in hand is but of vain affair,*

Presume it aught: what thou perceive is not!
Assume it naught: what thou conceive is there!
(Parchizadeh, 2010)

Making and sustaining peace requires creativity and a humanistic[11] approach to conflict resolution. Making and maintaining peace in the world depends on creative imagination, applying rationality, and valuing the moments of life for all in the world.

Of threats of Hell and Hopes of Paradise!
One thing at least is certain-This Life flies;
One thing is certain and the rest is Lies;
The Flower that once has blown for ever dies.
(Khayyam et al., 1997, p. 184)

Respecting the life of all in the world is a humanistic approach; it is important to reflect on transient life and its potency for creativity and possibility and apply rationality to see others hidden by the veil of established dogmas. The transcending nature of art and creativity makes it an essential instrument of peacemaking, as making peace often requires bridging the deep chasm of opposing forces. The value of time cannot be realized without peace, as violence inhibits creativity, disfigure beauty, and promote a reactionary attitude toward otherness. It demands immediate obedience rather than reflection and questioning.

Khayyam's poetry attests to his belief in rationality while acknowledging the limit of human rationality. It can be argued that applying a humanistic approach is required to make and maintain peace; however, it is by no means an assured path to distinguish the fire of violence and hatred. Showing humility in the face of the vast chest of secrets of the world is key to taming the hubris of rationality and science, which has been the cause of great suffering for humans.

Some look for truth in creeds, and forms, and rules
Some grope for doubts or dogmas in the schools

> *But from behind the veil a voice proclaims,*
> *"Your road lies neither here nor there, fools."*
> (Khayyam and Whinfield, 1980b, p. 252)

In the Khayyamian worldview, rationality and art are like the wings of the Phoenix that rise and save us from the hell of our dogma and certitude. Where rationality stops, the transcendent power of art removes the barriers and expands the creative space.

As Brian Eno (1996) said, "Rationality is what we do to organize the world, to make it possible to predict. Art is the rehearsal for the inapplicability and failure of that process" (p. 272).

Khayyam invites us to contemplate our existence and be multidimensional, artistic, and rational. Artists' inventiveness delivers what rationality is incapable of, creating possibilities from impossible. In the one-dimensional world trapped in the cycle of violence by its dogma and hubris, that would be our last hope.

> *O heart! can'st thou the darksome riddle read,*
> *Where wisest men have failed, wilt thou succeed?*
> *Quaff wine, and make thy heaven here below,*
> *Who knows if heaven above will be thy meed?*
> (Khayyam and Whinfield, 1980b, p. 286)

Notes

1. Translated by the author.
2. Richard Nelson Frye points to animosity toward Khayyam by Shams Tabrizi, Najm al-Din Daya, Al-Ghazali, and Attar, who "viewed Khayyam not as a fellow-mystic, but a free-thinking scientist."
3. Translated by the author.
4. Translated by the author.
5. Not to be confused with interactionism of Cartesian philosophy and the philosophy of mind.
6. Translated by the author.

7 Translated by the author.
8 Translated by the author.
9 Translated by the author.
10 Translated by the author.
11 Emmanuel Kant defined humanism as mankind coming to maturity through the practice of reason, supported through values and dignity.

CONCLUSION

Khayyam's worldview is timeless and relevant in the 21st century. His approach to human existential questions is brilliant, and his courage to face the dogmatic establishment of his era through the creative force of his art is commendable. Khayyam was born in a period when freethinking and rationality were under attack, from religious orthodoxies and mysticism. As a scientist and philosopher, Khayyam had to find a solution for the oppressive public space to challenge the shared beliefs and question the wisdom of established boundaries of knowledge. His strategy to overcome this challenge was nothing short of genius. Khayyam used his art to create and expand his creative space, where he, through the power of his potent poetry, not only challenged the established beliefs of his era but constructed a worldview that would lead humanity to excellence and fulfillment of its potential.

Khayyam used art to create a balance between science and philosophy; he stood at the cross section of science and art, where he used his poetry to expand the creative space and move the boundaries of knowledge.

He used the transcendental power of art to balance spirituality and rationality; Khayyam's spirituality stemmed from a sense of awe and wondered at the grand tapestry of creation and the essential existential mysteries of life. Khayyam spirituality is devoid of superstition and obedience to practices that subjugate life to the afterlife. In other words, his spirituality stemmed from his appreciation of creativity and art and their transcendental inspiration.

This approach is what the world needs today while the phony spiritual materialism has led humanity to meaninglessness and reinforcement of their ego.

Khayyam's worldview is the path to individuation that asks for total integration of all facets of the self and life: good and evil, and creation and death.

> *Source of joy and sorrow, We*
> *Reserve of justice, origin of tyranny, We*
> *Vile and pleasant, perfect and inferior, We*
> *Rusted mirror, Cup of Jamshid, We.*[1]

Khayyam sees life as temporal while lamenting its ephemerality; he urges us to value life's every moment by creating heaven on the earth. Khayyam strips life to its core, to get from superficial to significant; he lays bare the harsh reality of our existence, with all its anxieties and insecurities as well as potential and beauties.

In the Khayyamian worldview, life is an integration of its moments. Moments that emerge from interaction with beauty carry possibilities and have meaning; as Thomas Graham puts it in his review of Yukio Mishima's aesthetic sensibility, "beauty is most beautiful when it is transient" (Graham, 2020). Therefore, valuing moments requires making a choice; to choose who and what we connect and interact with and who to ignore. The assertion of the will to choose is central in building a meaningful path to happiness and joy.

Khayyam's path to happiness does not go through drunken stupors or the brothel; he is not an advocate for hedonism, and reading him with that lens is superficial. Having an aesthetic attitude toward life sharpens one's sense and alerts one's mind to be mindful of their choices. The choice is paramount in creating meaningful moments, as mindless repetition does not bear meaning and thus will not allow the moment to emerge. Therefore, those dwelling in a ritualistic way of life have a deficit of

CONCLUSION

moments in their life. Ritualization of life by either obedience to religious practices or mindless adhering to modern lifestyle is a recipe for a life that is monotonous and devoid of moments.

The question of God for Khayyam is to understand creativity as a mode of being. While in his philosophy, he is close to the mainstream view of omnipotent God, in his poetry, he challenges the same idea. His worldview is centered around understanding and expanding the boundaries of knowledge; he uses poetry as infantry to challenge and break through the heavily defended borders of beliefs and tradition.

Finding the inner balance between rationality and the transcendental power of art and creativity is vital. Khayyamian way of life is like walking on a tight rope, maintaining the balance between opposing forces in our life. Life begins with birth and ends with death; what we do with the moments that lie in the between is up to us.

Recognition of death as an end to conscious and subjective life is a sobering point in Khayyam's worldview. The transformative power of death is to turn the dead into the source of material for other life forms and bind the moments of life; mathematically speaking, death makes life a closed interval, with birth being the lower bound.

Thus to maximize the value of life, as Khayyam says, one has to make conscious choices to appreciate the value of its moment.

> *Child of four elements and sevenfold heaven,*
> *Who fume and sweat because of these eleven,*
> *Drink! I have told you seventy times and seven,*
> *Once gone, nor hell will send you back, nor heaven.*
> (Khayyam and Whinfield, 1980b, p. 288)

Khayyam project is human-centric and individualistic at its core. Focusing on the present moment and making conscious choices to avoid unnecessary suffering and expanding the creative space is an act of liberation. Khayyam's worldview promotes individual happiness and leads to a peaceful society through the enlightenment of its individual; it is an act of rebellion against the uniformity and herd mentality promoted by dogmatic ideologies and mechanistic way of life. The secret of joy lies in interaction and integration with the creative process, looking at the world from a creator's perspective, away from mental standardization imposed by stale institutions.

> *In slandering and reviling you persist,*
> *Calling me infidel and atheist:*
> *My errors I will not deny, but yet*
> *Does foul abuse become a moralist?*
>
> (Khayyam and Whinfield, 1980a, p. 302)

The Khayyamian worldview sets the foundation for a peaceful society; Khayyam's resistance against everydayness and mindless obedience is liberating; he asks us to make conscious choices about our lives and integrate and interact with beauty and creativity. Individuals enabled and enlightened to make conscious choices to enrich the moments of their life would not submit to the ideologies that promote violence and destruction. What allows tyrants to wage war and violence is the obedient populace, who, through forfeiting their free will and submitting to practices that promote ritualistic following, have fallen into the deindividuation (Postmes, 2001) machinery of tyranny.

While violence is deindividuating, art and creativity foster the sense of identity, making them the most significant barrier against tyranny. Peace is an act of creativity, like making art; it requires courage to go beyond the comfort of one dogma and entrenched beliefs. To make peace, we must first learn how to expand our creative space, recognize otherness, make room for them, and learn how to interact with them and a partner in imagining and creating new possibilities.

In his Nobel Prize acceptance lecture, "The Quest for Peace and Justice," Dr. Martin Luther King Jr. elegantly portrayed the role of creativity in peacemaking.:

> We must see that peace represents a sweeter music, a cosmic melody that is far superior to the discords of

CONCLUSION

war. Somehow, we must transform the dynamics of the world power struggle from the negative nuclear arms race, which no one can win, to a positive contest to harness man's creative genius to make peace and prosperity a reality for all of the nations of the world. In short, we must shift the arms race into a peace race. Suppose we have the will and determination to mount such a peace offensive. In that case, we will unlock hitherto tightly sealed doors of hope and transform our imminent cosmic elegy into a psalm of creative fulfillment.

(King, 1965)

Peace, like a symphony, requires the art of collaboration and innovation to expand the creative space for each performer to play and contribute to a shared purpose.

Peacebuilding is an art. Like art, it requires creative and free-thinking individuals; similar to music, it demands an imaginative composer who can construct and expand an inclusive creative space that fosters interaction and collaboration among individuals. Peace, similar to art, opens and expands humanity's worldview and enhances understanding of others, leading to empathy and inclusion. Through art, we can discover and see each other. The transcendental power of art moves beyond borders and cultural barriers; it preserves and promotes individuality while enhancing the sense of belonging. If art and peace are contingent upon the liberation of thought and creativity of the individual, violence is fueled by the deindividuation of the masses and curbing of creativity.

Agents of violent players are similar to slaves of the Zolian machine, subjugated to a mechanistic worldview that values them according to their function; their time is measured by the hands of the same clock that synchronizes the machine's output they operate and serve.

Generalization and reduction of individuals to the masses, where their values are supplanted by the unchallengeable rituals of the group ideology or traditions, is the first step toward turning them into a cog and slaves of Zolian machine-monster

CONCLUSION

(Zola, 1901). The machine-monster eventually devours its servants, like the mechanics of the engine in Zola's *The Monomaniac* humbling to their death under the wheels of the beast they were operating, carrying unassuming soldiers toward the frontline (Zola, 1901).

> It was the fortune, it was in a manner the doom, of Les Rougon-Mac-quart to deal with things almost always in gregarious form, to be a picture of numbers, of classes, crowds, confusions, movements. . . . The individual life is, if not wholly absent, reflected in coarse and common, in generalized terms.
> (Meadowsong, 2020)

The machine-monster takes many forms, from the religious orthodoxy of Khayyam's time to contemporary autocratic regimes and even the democratic institutions; despite their differences, all have the same deterministic path, only giving the impression of choice. At the same time, the track is fixed and the destination determined; the only choice is picking the window or aisle seat.

> *I could repent of all, but of wine, never!*
> *I could dispense with all, but with wine, never!*
> *If so be I became a Muslim,*
> *Could I abjure my Magian wine? no, never!*
> (Khayyam and Whinfield, 1980a, p. 280)

Humanity has built many iterations of machine monsters. In medieval times, the masters were the religious establishment; however, ideologies have supplanted the religious jurists with tyrants and demagogues in modern times. In the post-ideological politics of consensus, where democratic institutions have been reduced to social administration offices, the machine-monster has emerged differently. Politically nonexpressive consumers, with a pattern of behavior governed by imitation of social media influencers, give rise to hegemony of the generic (Badiou,

2005). Such masses are differentiated only by their way of consumption and affiliation to political parties. These parties converge to the prevailing demand of the atomized groups, which does not elevate much higher than their consumption habits.

A liberated person neither boards the machine-monster nor works as its engineer. To reconstruct the political sphere and decommission the engine of violence, first, the passengers need to become aware of their predicament.

Khayyamian worldview is constructed upon the idea of liberation from hegemony and dogma. It is necessary to educate the individual about the individuation process, where they can assert their choice over their temporal dimension and give meaning to their moments of life.

Khayyam should always be viewed as an equilibrist walking on a tightrope between the dogma of religious authority and the superstition of mysticism. He maintained a balance between his work and extraordinary life through science, philosophy, and art. To derail the machine-monster of our era, we need to walk the same tightrope, using art to expand the creative space and challenging the boundaries of our knowledge and tradition while utilizing science and philosophy to give order and make sense of the new envisioned possibility.

In a lone waste I saw a debauchee,
He had no home, no faith, no heresy,
No God, no truth, no law, no certitude
Where in this world is man so bold as he?
(Khayyam and Whinfield, 1980a, p. 252).

Khayyam's project is a personal one. He questioned the foundational assumptions of the world, and when his science and philosophy fell short, he summoned art to his assistance. Khayyam shows us how the interaction and convergence with beauty expand the creative space and resurrect the art's disruptive and innovative potential to create new possibilities. It is the convergence with art that gives meaning to our moments and leads to the emergence of time.[2]

CONCLUSION

In Khayyam's work, the echoes of other philosophers, in particular stoics, can be heard, like this passage from Marcus Aurelius's *Meditations*:

> Mark how fleeting and paltry is the estate of man, yesterday in embryo, tomorrow a mummy or ashes. So for the hairsbreadth of time assigned to thee, live rationally, and part with life cheerfully, as drops the ripe olive, extolling the season that bore it and the tree that matured it.
>
> (Aurelius, 1942)

Khayyam did not prescribe a way of life to become happier. He asks us to be aware of our choices and the boundaries of our life, particularly birth and death. There is no choice in birth, and death is all but certain; however, we have full sovereignty over our time. Khayyam ridicules trading the excitement of life with a promise of a dull afterlife, rightfully so; as for a creative mind, the idea of endless temporal life possibilities is more attractive than the immutability of eternity.

> *Who e'er returned of all that went before,*
> *To tell of that long road they travel o'er?*
> *Leave naught undone of what you have to do,*
> *For when you go, you will return no more.*
> (Khayyam and Whinfield, 1980a, p. 174)

Reading Khayyam today teaches us that the path of liberation is a personal one and freedom of thought is the ultimate form of liberation as the choice is contingent on unbounded creativity. Attuning happiness and joy in the Khayyamian world depends on choice and freedom to move boundaries of beliefs and knowledge. Khayyam's message is clear—rather than becoming an obedient subject of ideological or theological dogma, take the path of creativity and liberation from a prescribed way of life and live rationally and creatively. In a sense, he invites us to walk the tightrope of spirituality without falling

CONCLUSION

into the trap of mysticism or religious dogma. Khayyam's art is spiritual and yet rational. He used his art as a vehicle to develop and express his spirituality in an era where deviation from subscribed path to heaven had dire consequences.

> *Who e'er returned of all that went before,*
> *To tell of that long road they travel o'er?*
> *Leave naught undone of what you have to do,*
> *For when you go, you will return no more.*
>
> (Whinfield p. 141)

Khayyam's approach to art echoes throughout history. As Kandinsky puts it in his 1912 booklet, *Concerning the Spiritual in Art*:

> When religion, science and morality are shaken (the last by the strong hand of Nietzsche) and when outer supports threaten to fall, man withdraws his gaze from externals and turns it inwards. Literature, music and art are the most sensitive spheres in which this spiritual revolution makes itself felt. They reflect the dark picture of the present time and show the importance of what was at first only a little point of light noticed by the few. Perhaps they even grow dark in their turn, but they turn away from the soulless life of the present toward those substances and ideas that give free scope to the non-material strivings of the soul.
>
> (Kandinsky and Sadleir, 2008)

Khayyam's balance of work provides a guiding principle on how to be, live, and find meaning in the world full of echo chambers of dogma, filled with cacophony and endless opinionating. His life and work show us how to face life's difficult questions without settling for lazy answers, sold by merchants of religion and packaged spiritualities. To maintain a careful balance between science, philosophy, and art in uncertain times, all while pushing the boundaries of established beliefs, required immense courage. He was the most notable intellectual rebel of his era, not only because he stood up against the orthodox jurists and dismissed the asceticism of mystics but also the way he illuminated the path of enlightenment for many generations to come.

> *Assume, eludes you the secrets of the universe*
> *And Remote is the wise technique*
> *Rise and raise a paradise from wine and green*
> *As in heaven, you may arrive or not.*[3]

Notes

1. Translated by the author.
2. Jackson Pollock's statement on his painting: "When I am my painting, I'm not aware of what I'm doing. It is only after a sort of "get acquainted" period that I see what I have been about. I have no feels about making changes, destroying the image, etc., because the painting has a life of its own I try to let it come through. It is only when I lose contact with the painting that the result is a mess. Otherwise, there is pure harmony, an easy give and take, and the painting comes out well. The source of my painting is unconscious."
3. Translated by the author.

APPENDIX

A Stylometric Analysis of Khayyam's Poetry

Stylometry (Savoy, 2020) is the quantitative study of literary style by the identification of its features of style (Finn and Kushmerick, 2003). It allows measuring the style of the author by using statistical analysis to identify features of style (Reddy et al., 2016). The authorship of many quartets in Rubaiyat has always been a point of contention, making a good candidate for stylometric analysis and author attribution techniques (Antosch, 1969).

To train the model and find author's unique style and using an authentic source, poems analyzed by Iranian experts such as Mohammad Ali Foroughi has been used.

Ridge regression (Hoerl and Kennard, 1970) was used to determine the most "predictive" words for Khayyam quartets. Then building a training and test data set, the model was trained to predict the authorship of disputed quartets.

The following quartet was selected for analysis by the model:

آنی که نبودت به خور و خواب نیاز
کردند نیازمندت این چار نیاز
هر یک به تو آنچه داد بستاند باز
تا باز چنان شوی که بودی ز آغاز

هنگام صبوح ای صنم فرخ پی
برساز ترانه‌ای و پیش‌آور می
کافکند بخاک صد هزاران جم و کی
این آمدن تیرمه و رفتن دی

A STYLOMETRIC ANALYSIS OF KHAYYAM'S POETRY

هان کوزه گرا بپای اگر هشیاری
تا چند کنی بر گل مردم خواری
انگشت فریدون و کف کیخسرو
بر چرخ نهاده ای چه می‌پنداری

گر کار فلک به عدل سنجیده بدی
احوال فلک جمله پسندیده بدی
ور عدل بدی بکارها در گردون
کی خاطر اهل فضل رنجیده بدی

گر دست دهد ز مغز گندم نانی
وز می دو منی ز گوسفندی رانی
با لاله رخی و گوشه بستانی
عیشی بود آن نه حد هر سلطانی

گر آمدنم بخود بدی نامدمی
ور نیز شدن بمن بدی کی شدمی
به زان نبدی که اندر این دیر خراب
نه آمدمی نه شدمی نه بدمی

زان کوزه می که نیست در وی ضرری
پر کن قدحی بخور بمن ده دگری
زان پیشتر ای صنم که در رهگذری
خاک من و تو کوزه کند کوزه گری

در گوش دلم گفت فلک پنهانی
حکمی که قضا بود ز من میدانی
در گردش خویش اگر مرا دست بدی
خود را بر هاندمی ز سرگردانی

در کارگه کوزه گری کردم رای
در پایه چرخ دیدم استاد بپای
میکرد دلیر کوزه را دسته و سر
از کله پادشاه و از دست گدای

خوش باش که پخته‌اند سودای تو دی
فارغ شده‌اند از تمنای تو دی

111

قصه چه کنم که به تقاضای تو دی
دادند قرار کار فردای تو دی

چندان که نگاه می‌کنم هر سویی
در باغ روان است ز کوثر جویی
صحرا چو بهشت است ز کوثر کم گوی
بنشین به بهشت با بهشتی رویی

تا چند حدیث پنج و چار ای ساقی
مشکل چه یکی چه صد هزار ای ساقی
خاکیم همه چنگ بساز ای ساقی
بادیم همه باده بیار ای ساقی

پیری دیدم به خانه خماری
گفتم نکنی ز رفتگان اخباری
گفتا می خور که همچو ما بسیاری
رفتند و خبر باز نیامد باری

آن قصر که جمشید در آن جام گرفت
آهو بچه کرد و روبه آرام گرفت
بهرام که گور می گرفتی همه عمر
دیدی که چگونه گور، بهرام گرفت؟

قرآن که مهین کلام خوانند آن را
گه گاه نه بر دوام خوانند آن را
بر گرد پیاله آیتی هست مقیم
کاندر همه جا مدام خوانند آن را

بر چهره‌ی گل نسیم نوروز خوش است
بر صحن چمن روی دل افروز خوش است
از دی که گذشت هر چه گویی خوش نیست
خوش باش و ز دی مگو که امروز خوش است

روزی است خوش و هوا نه گرم است و نه سرد
ابر از رخ گلزار همی شوید گرد
بلبل به زبان حال خود با گل زرد
فریاد همی زند که می باید خورد

تا کی عمرت به خودپرستی گذرد؟
یا در پی نیستی و هستی گذرد؟
می خور که چنین عمر که مرگ از پس اوست
آن به که به خواب یا به مستی گذرد

این عقل که در ره سعادت پوید
روزی صد بار، خود تو را می گوید
دریاب تو این یک دم عمرت که نه ای
آن تره که بدروند و از سر روید

هر سبزه که برکنار جویی رسته است
گویی ز لب فرشته خویی رسته است
پا بر سر هر سبزه بخواری ننهی
کان سبزه ز خاک لاله رویی رسته است

می خور که به زیر گل بسی خواهی خفت
بی مونس و بی رفیق و بی همدم و جفت
زنهار به کس مگو تو این راز نهفت
هر لاله که پژمرد نخواهد بشکفت

گویند که دوزخی بود عاشق و مست
قولی است خلاف؛ دل در او نتوان بست
گر عاشق و مست، دوزخی خواهد بود
فردا بینی بهشت همچون کف دست

گردون نگری ز قد فرسوده ی ماست
جیحون اثری ز اشک آلوده ی ماست
دوزخ شرری ز رنج بیهوده ی ماست
فردوس دمی ز وقت آسوده ی ماست

ساقی گل و سبزه بس طربناک شده است
دریاب که هفته ی دگر خاک شده است
می نوش و گلی بچین که تا درنگری
گل خاک شده است و سبزه خاشاک شده است

گر از پی شهرت و هوا خواهی رفت
از من خبرت که بی نوا خواهی رفت

بنگر که که ای و از کجا آمده ای
می دان که چه می کنی کجا خواهی رفت

ساقی، غم من برون ز اندازه شده است
سرمستی من برون ز اندازه شده است
با موی سپید سرخوشم کز خط تو
پیرانه سرم بهار دل تازه شده است

چون عهده نمیشود کسی فردا را
حالی خوش کن تو این دل شیدا را
می نوش به ماهتاب ای ماه که ماه
بسیار بتابد و نتابد ما را

آمد سحری ندا ز میخانه ی ما
کای رند خراباتی دیوانه ی ما
بر خیز که پر کنیم پیمانه ز می
زان پیش که پر کنند پیمانه ی ما

ترکیب طبایع چون به کام تو دمی است
رو شاد بزی اگر چه بر تو ستمی است
با اهل خرد باش که اصل تن تو
گردی و نسیمی و غباری و دمی است

می خور که سمن بسی سپا خواهد شد
خوش زی که سهی، بسی سها خواهد شد
بر طرف چمن ز زندگانی برخور
زیرا که چمن چو ما بسی خواهد شد

The predicted attributed all but the following two quartet to Khayyam,

گر از پی شهرت و هوا خواهی رفت
از من خبرت که بی نوا خواهی رفت
بنگر که که ای و از کجا آمده ای
می دان که چه می کنی کجا خواهی رفت

آمد سحری ندا ز میخانه ی ما
کای رند خراباتی دیوانه ی ما
بر خیز که پر کنیم پیمانه ز می
زان پیش که پر کنند پیمانه ی ما

It is important that while stylometric analysis of Khayyam quartets provides useful insight into author attribution, it should be used in conjunction with historical and literary analysis of the poems.

The analysis and data can be found at https://github.com/nloghmani/khayyam.

REFERENCES

Aminrazavi, Mehdi. (2007). *The Wine of Wisdom: The Life, Poetry and Philosophy of Omar Khayyam.* Oneworld Publications.

Aminrazavi, M. and Brummelen, G. V. (2017). Umar Khayyam. In E. N. Zalta (Ed.), *The Stanford Encyclopedia of Philosophy* (Spring 2017 ed). Stanford University. Retrieved September 12, 2020, from https://plato.stanford.edu/entries/umar-khayyam/

Anter, A. (2020). The Modern State and Its Monopoly on Violence. In E. Hanke, L. Scaff, and S. Whimster (Eds.), *The Oxford Handbook of Max Weber.* Oxford University Press.

Antosch, F. (1969). The Diagnosis of Literary Style with the Verb-Adjective Ratio. In L. Dolezel and R. W. Bailey (Eds.), *Statistics and Style.* American Elsevier.

Arendt, H. (1970). *Men in Dark Times.* HMH Books.

Arendt, H., and Kohn, J. (2006). *Between Past and Future.* Penguin Publishing Group.

Ariès, P., Duby, G., and Goldhammer, A. (1987). *A History of Private Life: Revelations of the Medieval World.* Belknap Press of Harvard University Press.

Aurelius, Marcus, Emperor of Rome, 121–180. (1942). *The Meditations.* Peter Pauper Press.

Awn, J. P. (1983). The Ethical Concerns of Classical Sufism. *The Journal of Religious Ethics*, 11(2), 240–263.

Backman, Clifford R. (2009). *The Worlds of Medieval Europe.* Oxford University Press.

Badiou, A. (2005). Politics: A Non-Expressive Dialectics. Paper presented at Is the Politics of Truth Still Thinkable? BIH.

REFERENCES

Bell, C. (1992). *Ritual Theory, Ritual Practice* (p. 74). Oxford University Press.

Bell, C. (1997). *Ritual: Perspectives and Dimensions* (pp. 139–140). Oxford University Press.

Benson, C. (1993). *The Absorbed Self: Pragmatism, Psychology and Aesthetic Experience*. Harvester Wheatsheaf.

Bercovitch, S. (2014). *The Rites of Assent: Transformations in the Symbolic Construction of America* (p. 312). Routledge.

Bergson, H. (2016). *Time and Free Will: An Essay on the Immediate Data of Consciousness* (199–201). Lulu.com.

Bīrūnī, M. A., and Sachau, E. (1879). *The Chronology of Ancient Nations: An English Version of the Arabic Text of the Athâr-ul-Bâkiya of Albîrûni Or "Vestiges of the Past"*. William H. Allen & Company.

Black, A. (2011). *The History of Islamic Political Thought*. Edinburgh University Press.

Bolt, M., Hockey, T., Palmeri, J. A., Trimble, V., Williams, T. R., Bracher, K., Jarrell, R., Marché, J. D., and Ragep, F. J. (2007). *Biographical Encyclopedia of Astronomers*. Springer New York.

Bosworth, C. (1975). The Early Ghaznavids. In R. Frye (Ed.), *The Cambridge History of Iran* (pp. 162–197). Cambridge University Press.

Boyer, C. B. (1988). *History of Analytic Geometry*. The Scholar's Bookshelf.

Boyle, J. A. (1969). *Omar Khayyam: Astronomer, Mathematician and Poet*. John Rylands Libr.

Brandon, S. (2017). Salvation. In *Encyclopædia Britannica*. Retrieved September 29, 2020, from www.britannica.com/topics/Salvation

Brett, M. (2017). *The Fatimid Empire*. Edinburgh University Press.

Britannica, T. Editors of Encyclopaedia. (2013, June 20). Asceticism. In *Encyclopedia Britannica*. https://www.britannica.com/topic/asceticism

Britannica, T. Editors of Encyclopaedia (2013, August 2). Heian Period. In *Encyclopedia Britannica*. https://www.britannica.com/event/Heian-period

Britannica, T. Editors of Encyclopaedia. (2018, May 29). Nishapur Pottery. In *Encyclopedia Britannica*. Retrieved December 2021 from https://www.britannica.com/art/Nishapur-pottery.

REFERENCES

Britannica, T. Editors of Encyclopaedia. (2021, December 1). Sri Aurobindo. In *Encyclopedia Britannica*. Retrieved December 16, 2021, from https://www.britannica.com/biography/Sri-Aurobindo.

Brockhaus, H. (2018, September 28). Pope Stresses Peace in Unscheduled Meeting with Burma's Religious Leaders. *Catholic News Agency*. Retrieved October 16, 2020, from https://www.catholicnewsagency.com/news/37275/pope-stresses-peace-in-unscheduled-meeting-with-burmas-religious-leaders

Brooks, D. (2017, December 14). The Glory of Democracy. *The New York Times*. www.nytimes.com/2017/12/14/opinion/democracy-thomas-mann.html

Browne, E. G. (1959). *A Literary History of Persia* (Vol. 4). Cambridge University Press.

Carnap, R. (1963). Carnap's Intellectual Biography. In P. A. Schilpp (Ed.), *The Philosophy of Rudolf Carnap* (pp. 3–84). La Salle.

Clark, T. J. (1973). *Image of the People: Gustave Courbet and the Second French Republic, 1848–1851* (p. 252). New York Graphic Society.

Colgan, R. (2009). *Advice to the Young Physician: On the Art of Medicine*. Springer.

Cross, F. L., and Livingstone, E. A. (2005). *The Oxford Dictionary of the Christian Church*. Oxford University Press.

Daryaee, T. (2020). *Wine Good and Fine: The Art of Wine in Ancient Persia*. CAIS: The Circle of Ancient Iranian Studies. Retrieved December 18, 2020 from www.cais-soas.com/CAIS/Culture/wine_good.htm

Dasch, E. J., and O'Meara, S. J. (Eds.). (2018). *A Dictionary of Space Exploration*. Oxford University Press.

Deng, N. (2018). Eternity in Christian Thought. In E. N. Zalta (Ed.), *Stanford Encyclopedia of Philosophy*. Retrieved January 12, 2021, from https://plato.stanford.edu/archives/fall2018/entries/eternity/

Dewey, J. (1934). *Art as Experience*. Penguin.

Diffey, J. T. (1994). Art and the Transcendent. *The British Journal of Aesthetics*, *34*(4), 326–336.

Dod, B. (1982). Aristoteles Latinus. In N. Kretzmann, A. Kenny, J. Pinborg, and E. Stump (Eds.), *The Cambridge History of Later Medieval Philosophy: From the Rediscovery of Aristotle to the Disintegration of Scholasticism, 1100–1600* (pp. 43–79). Cambridge University Press.

Dreyfus, H., and Wrathall, M. (Eds.). (2002). *Authenticity, Death, and the History of Being: Heidegger Reexamined*. Routledge.

Dreyfus, H., and Wrathall, M. (Eds.). (2005). *A Companion to Heidegger*. Blackwell.

REFERENCES

Druart, T.-A. (2020, Fall). Al-Farabi. In E. N. Zalta (Ed.), *The Stanford Encyclopedia of Philosophy*. Metaphysics Research Lab, Stanford University. https://plato.stanford.edu/archives/fall2020/entries/al-farabi/

Eckhard, M. (1999). The Ottonians as Kings and Emperors. In T. Timothy Reuter (Ed.), *The New Cambridge Medieval History, Volume 3: c.900—c.1024* (pp. 233–266). Cambridge University Press.

Elman, B. A. (2013). *Civil Examinations and Meritocracy in Late Imperial China*. Harvard University Press.

Emerson, R. W., Ferguson, A. R., Slater, J., Carr, J. F., and Spiller, R. (Eds.). (1971). *The Collected Work of Ralph Waldo Emerson*. Harvard University Press.

Eno, B. (1996). *A Year with Swollen Appendices* (p. 272). Fabe & Faber.

Evans, B., and Bernstein, R. (2017, January 26). The Intellectual Life of Violence. *The New York Times*. www.nytimes.com

Farābī, A. N. M. I. M., Mahdi, M., Butterworth, C. E., and Pangle, T. L. (2001). *Alfarabi: Philosophy of Plato and Aristotle*. Cornell University Press. https://books.google.co.in/books?id=-SaXczxPo40C

Fiegenbaum, J. W. (2018). *Al-Ḥallāj, Religious Personages & Scholars Encyclopedia Articles*. Encyclopedia Britannica. www.britannica.com/biography/al-Hallaj

Finn, A., and Kushmerick, N. (2003). Learning to Classify Documents According to Genre. In S. Argamon (Ed.), *IJCAI-03 Workshop on Computational Approaches to Style Analysis and Synthesis*. Wiley.

Fisher, J. (1974). Destruction as a Mode of Creation. *Journal of Aesthetic Education*, 8(2), 64.

FitzGerald, E. (1997). *Edward FitzGerald, Rubáiyát of Omar Khayyám*. University Press of Virginia.

Flannery, K. L. S. J. (2001). *Acts Amid Precepts: The Logical Structure of Thomas Aquinas's Moral Theology*. Bloomsbury Academic.

Floor, Willem (2005). PAPER ii. Paper and Papermaking. In *Encyclopædia Iranica*, online edition. Retrieved 16 August 2017 from http://www.iranicaonline.org/articles/paper-and-papermaking.

Foroughi, Mohammad Ali. [Rubaiyat of Khayyam, corrected edition], رباعیات خیام - متن درست و کامل رباعیات اصیل خیام با مقابلۀ نسخه تصحیح مرحوم محمدعلی فروغی Tehran, Amir Kabir, 1976.

Frankopan, P. (2015). *The Silk Roads: A New History of the World*. Bloomsbury Publishing.

Frye, R. N. (1975). *The Cambridge History of Iran* (Vol. 4). Cambridge University Press.

REFERENCES

Garakani, Gharaee and Brown, Keven (2013). "*Bahmanyār b. al-Marzubān*". In Wilferd Madelung and Daftary Wilferd (Eds.), *Encyclopaedia Islamica Online*. Brill Online.

Gascoigne, N. (2013). *Richard Rorty*. Polity Press.

George, Saliba (2020, August 31). Al-Bīrūnī. In *Encyclopedia Britannica*. Retrieved October 20, 2020, from https://www.britannica.com/biography/al-Biruni

Germann, N. (2016). Al-Farabi's Philosophy of Society and Religion. https://plato.stanford.edu/archives/win2019/entries/al-farabi-soc-rel/

Geroch, R. (1981). *General Relativity From A to B*. University of Chicago Press.

Ginsborg, H. (2005). Kant's Aesthetics and Teleology. In E. N. Zalta (Ed.), *The Stanford Encyclopedia of Philosophy* (Winter 2019 ed.). Stanford University Press.

Gleiser, M. (2013, March 27). The Origin of The Universe: From Nothing Everything? *npr*. www.npr.org/sections/13.7/2013/03/26/175352714/the-origin-of-the-universe-from-nothing-everything

Gordon, H. (2000). *Dwelling Poetically*. Brill | Rodopi.

Graham, T. (2020, November 24). Yukio Mishima: The Strange Tale of Japan's Infamous Novelist. *BBC*. www.bbc.com/culture/article/20201124-yukio-mishima-the-strange-tale-of-japans-infamous-novelist

Gutas, D. (2011). AVICENNA ii. Biography. In *Encyclopædia Iranica*, III/1, pp. 67–70. Retrieved October 20, 2020, from http://www.iranicaonline.org/articles/avicenna-ii (accessed on 20 October 2020).

Guthrie, S. E. (1993). *Faces in the Clouds: A New Theory of Religion*. Oxford University Press.

Guthrie, S. E. (2008). Anthropomorphism. In *Encyclopædia Britannica*. Retrieved December 7, 2020, from www.britannica.com/topics/anthropomorphism

Hendrix, S. L. (2005). *Aesthetics & the Philosophy of Spirit*. Peter Lang.

Heraclitus. (2017). *Heraclitus on the Two Antithetical Forces in Life: Interdependent and Mutually Convertible Aspects of One Cause*. Philaletheians.

Heron-Allen, E., Whinfield, E. H., Nicolas, J. B., and FitzGerald, E. (1908). *The Sufistic Quatrains of Omar Khayyam in Definitive Form* (p. 244). United States: Wiley.

Hill, E. T. (1980). Humanity as an End in Itself. *Ethics*, 91(1), 84–99.

Hoerl, A., and Kennard, R. (1970). Ridge Regression: Biased Estimation for Nonorthogonal Problems. *Technometrics*, 12(1), 55–67.

REFERENCES

Hongladarom, S., and Joaquin, J. J. (2021). *Love and Friendship Across Cultures*. Springer.

Honigmann, E., and Bosworth, C. E. (n.d.). NISHAPUR. In *Encyclopaedia of Islam* (2nd ed., p. VIII:62b). Brill. https://referenceworks.brillonline.com:443/entries/encyclopaedia-of-islam-2/nishapur-SIM_5930

Horne, C. F. (1917). *The Sacred Books and Early Literature of the East: With an Historical Survey and Descriptions* (Vol. 8, pp. 13–14). Parke, Austin & Lipscomb.

Insler, S. (1975). *The Gathas of Zarathustra*. E.J. Brill.

Jahanbegloo, R. (2020). *Albert Camus: The Unheroic Hero of Our Time*. Routledge India.

Janin, H. (2014). *The University in Medieval Life, 1179–1499*. McFarland, Incorporated, Publishers.

Jung, C. (1966). *Two Essays on Analytical Psychology*. Princeton University Press.

Kalar, B. (2006). *Demands of Taste in Kant's Aesthetics*. Continuum International Publishing Group.

Kandinsky, W., and Sadleir, M. (2008). *Concerning the Spiritual in Art*. Floating Press.

Kant, I. (1784). *Groundwork of the Metaphysics of Morals*. Cambridge University Press.

Kant, I. (1999). *Practical Philosophy* (Mary J. Gregor, Trans.) (p. 17). Cambridge University Press.

Kant, I., and Smith, M. C. (n.d.). What Is Enlightenment? In *Columbia.edu*. Retrieved October 10, 2020, from www.columbia.edu/acis/ets/CCREAD/etscc/kant.html#note1

Katouzian, H. (1991). *Sadeq Hedayat: The Life and Literature of an Iranian Writer*. Palgrave Macmillan.

Khaleghi-Motlagh, Djalal (2012, January 26). Ferdowsi, Abu'l Qāsem i. Life. In *Encyclopædia Iranica*. Vol. IX, Fasc. 5, pp. 514–523. Retrieved October 22, 2020, from https://iranicaonline.org/articles/ferdowsi-i

Khayyam, O. (1070). *Treatise on Demonstrations of Problems of Algebra*.

Khayyam, O., Decker, C., and FitzGerald, E. (1997). *Edward FitzGerald, Rubáiyát of Omar Khayyám: A Critical Edition*. University Press of Virginia.

Khayyam, O., and FitzGerald, E. (1910). *Rubaiyat of Omar Khayyam*. Selfridge & Co.

REFERENCES

Khayyam, O., FitzGerald, E., Heron-Allen, E., Whinfield, E., Nicolas, J. B., and Arnot, R. (Eds.). (1903). *The Sufistic quatrains of Omar Khayyám*. M. Walter Dunne.

Khayyam, O., FitzGerald, E., Whinfield, E., McCarthy, J. H., and Rittenhouse, J. B. (1940). *The Rubaiyat of Omar Khayyam: Comprising the Metrical Translations by Edward FitzGerald and E. H. Whinfield and the Prose Version of Justin Huntly McCarthy*. T. Nelson.

Khayyam, O., and Heron-Allen, E. (1898). *The Ruba', yat of Omar Khayyām: Being a Facsimile of the Manuscript in the Bodleian Library at Oxford, with a Transcript into Modern Persian Characters*. L.C. Page.

Khayyam, O., and Whinfield, E. H. (1883). *The Quatrains of Omar Khayyam* (p. 302).

Khayyam, O., and Whinfield, E. H. (1980a). *The Quatrains of Omar Khayyám*. Octagon Press.

Khayyam, O., and Whinfield, E. H. (1980b). *The Quatrains of Omar Khayyám: The Persian Text with an English Verse Translation*. Published for the Sufi Trust by the Octagon Press.

Kimball, C. (2002). *When Religion Becomes Evil* (p. 72). HarperCollins.

King, M. L. (1965). *Nobel Lecture by the Reverend Dr. Martin Luther King, Jr: Recipient of the 1964 Nobel Peace Prize, Oslo, Norway, December 11, 1964*. Clarke & Way.

Klein, A. (2012). *The Art of Living Joyfully: How to be Happier Every Day of the Year*. Viva Editions.

Lanier, A. R. (2017). Friedrich Nietzsche. In E. N. Zalta (Ed.), *Stanford Encyclopedia of Philosophy*. Retrieved October 15, 2020, from https://plato.stanford.edu/archives/sum2017/entries/nietzsche/.

Lee, B. (2001). *Artist of life* (J. Little, Ed.). Tuttle Publishing.

Lindberg, D. C. (1976). *Theories of Vision from al-Kindi to Kepler*. University Press.

Lyons, M. (2013). *Books: A Living History*. Thames & Hudson.

Maddison, A. (2001). *The World Economy: A Millennial Perspective*. Development Centre Studies, OECD Publishing. https://doi.org/10.1787/9789264189980-en.

Malcolm, J. (2011). *The History of Persia: From the Most Early Period to the Present Time* (Cambridge Library Collection – Travel, Middle East and Asia Minor, pp. 12–30, 221–222, Chapter VIII). Cambridge University Press. doi:10.1017/CBO9780511983177.004

Mann, T. (1937). *An Exchange of Letters*. A. A. Knopf.

Mann, T. (1942). *Order of the Day: Political Essays and Speeches of Two Decades*. A. A. Knopf.

REFERENCES

Mansouri, R. (2013). The History of Science in Iran from a Physicist's Perspective. In A. S. Soofi and S. Ghazinoory (Eds.), *Science and Innovations in Iran: Development, Progress, and Challenges* (pp. 15–38). Palgrave Macmillan.

Mardia K. V. (2004). Omar Khayyam, René Descartes and Solutions to Algebraic Equations. In I. G. Guinness and B. S. Yadav (Eds.), *History of the Mathematical Sciences* (pp. 135–148). Hindustan Book Agency. https://doi.org/10.1007/978-93-86279-16-3_11

Martin, M. (1997). Problems with Heaven. In M. Martin and K. Augustine (Eds.), *The Myth of an Afterlife: The Case Against Life After Death*. Rowman & Littlefield.

McWhorter, Ladelle, and Gail Stenstad (Eds.) (2009). *Heidegger and the Earth: Essays in Environmental Philosophy*. University of Toronto Press. https://doi.org/10.3138/9781442697720

Meadowsong, Z. E. (2020). *Narrative Machine: The Naturalist, Modernist, and Postmodernist Novel*. Routledge.

Merriam-Webster. (n.d.). Sommelier. In *Merriam-Webster.com Dictionary*. Retrieved September 22, 2020, from www.merriam-webster.com/dictionary/sommelier

Moon, Ban Ki. (2012, September 12). *Remarks at the Opening of the Exhibit of the Chinese Artist, Wu Weishan*. United Nations Secretary-General.www.un.org/sg/en/content/sg/speeches/2012-09-04/remarks-opening-exhibit-chinese-artist-wu-weishan

Morgan, D. (1976). Richard N. Frye: The Golden Age of Persia: The Arabs in the East. (History of Civilisation.) xiii, 290 pp., 16 Plates. London: Weidenfeld and Nicolson, [1975]. £7. *Bulletin of the School of Oriental and African Studies, 39*(1), 179–180. doi:10.1017/S0041977X00052319

Muhling, K. (2020). Immutability. In *Reformed Answers*. Retrieved September 20, 2020, from http://reformedanswers.org/answer.asp/file/40331

Nasr, S. H. (1993). *An Introduction to Islamic Cosmological Doctrines*. State University of New York Press.

Needham, J., and Ronan, C. A. (1978). *The Shorter Science and Civilisation in China: Volume 4*. Cambridge University Press.

Nietzsche, F., and Kaufmann, W. (1978). *Thus Spoke Zarathustra*. Penguin Books.

Parchizadeh, R. (2010). *The Persian Popular Songs, Attributed to Xayam*. Zaban Ketab.

Pearsall, J. (1998). Pantheist. In J. Pearsall and P. Hanks (Eds.), *The New Oxford Dictionary of English* (pp. 1341). Clarendon Press.

REFERENCES

Pope, A. (1733). *An Essay on Man*. Samuel R. Wells.

Popkin, R. H. (2020, November 18). Skepticism. In *Encyclopedia Britannica*. Retrieved December 16, 2021, from https://www.britannica.com/topic/skepticism

Postmes, T. (2001). Psychology of Deindividuation. In N. J. Smelser and P. B. Baltes (Eds.), *International Encyclopedia of the Social & Behavioral Sciences* (pp. 3364–3366). Pergamon. ISBN 9780080430768. https://doi.org/10.1016/B0-08-043076-7/01803-9

Ranciere, J. (1991). *The Ignorant Schoolmaster: Five Lessons in Intellectual Emancipation*. Stanford University Press (Original work published 1987).

Rāshid, R., and Vahabzadeh, B. (2000). *Omar Khayyam, the Mathematician*. Bibliotheca Persica Press.

Reddy, T. R., Vardhan, V. B., and Reddy, P. V. (2016). A Survey on Authorship Profiling Techniques. *International Journal of Applied Engineering Research*, 11(5), 3092–3102.

Rosenfeld, B. A., and Youschkevitch, A. P. (1973). Al-Khayyāmī. In C. C. Gillispie (Ed.), *Dictionary of Scientific Biography* (16 vols., VII, pp. 323–334).

Ross, E. D., and Gibb, H. A. R. (1929). *The Earliest Account of Umar Khayyam*. Cambridge University Press.

Saunders, K. J. (1947). *A Pageant of India*. Oxford University Press.

Savoy, J. (2020). *Machine Learning Methods for Stylometry: Authorship Attribution and Author Profiling*. Springer International Publishing.

Seneca, L. A. (2005). *On the Shortness of Life* (C. D. Costa, Trans.). Penguin Books.

Shen, F. (1996). *Cultural Flow between China and Outside World Throughout History/Shen Fuwei* (1st ed., Wu Jingshu Trans.). Foreign Languages Press.

Shepard, W. E. (2021). *Introducing Islam*. Routledge.

Sherman, N. (1999). *Aristotle's Ethics: Critical Essays*. Rowman & Littlefield Publishers.

Sjöholm, C. (2015). *Doing Aesthetics with Arendt: How to See Things*. Columbia University Press.

Spinks, L. (2010). Active/Reactive. In *The Deleuze Dictionary*. Retrieved September 30, 2020, from https://deleuze.enacademic.com/4

Strousma, S. (1999). Abū Bakr Al-Rāzī: A "Respectable" Freethinker. In *Freethinkers of Medieval Islam: Ibn Al-Rawāndī, Abū Bakr Al-Rāzī and Their Impact on Islamic Thought* (pp. 87–92). Brill.

REFERENCES

Struik, D. J. (1958). Omar Khayyam, Mathematician. *The Mathematics Teacher*, 51(4), 280–285. http://www.jstor.org/stable/27955652

Swanton, C. (2015). *The Virtue Ethics of Hume and Nietzsche*. Wiley Blackwell.

Sweet, S. A., Fliegstein, N., and Sandholtz, W. (2001). The Institutionalization of European Space. In S. A. Sweet, N. Fliegstein, and W. Sandholtz (Eds.), *The Institutionalization of Europe* (pp. 12). Oxford University Press.

Timpe, K. (2013). *Free Will in Philosophical Theology*. Bloomsbury Publishing.

Tirtha, S. G. and Khayyam, O. (1941). *The Nectar of Grace: Omar Khayyām's Life and Works*. Kitabistan.

Vogt, K. (2018). Ancient Skepticism. In E. N. Zalta (Ed.), *Stanford Encyclopedia of Philosophy*. Stanford University. https://plato.stanford.edu/archives/fall2018/entries/skepticism-ancient/

Wallace, D. F. (2014). *The David Foster Wallace Reader*. Penguin Random House Australia.

Whaley, J. (2018). *The Holy Roman Empire: A Very Short Introduction*. Oxford University Press.

Whinfield, E. (1893). *The Quatrains of Omar Khayyám* (p. 89). K. Paul, Trench, Trübner & Company. Modified by the Author.

Whinfield, E. (2013). *The Quatrains of Omar Khayyam*. Taylor & Francis.

World Health Organization. (1999). *Injury: A Leading Cause of the Global Burden of Disease*. Geneva.

Xiao-bin, J. (2003). Mirror for Government: Ssu-ma Kuang's Thought on Politics and Government in Tzu-chih t'ung-chien. In T. H. C. Lee (Ed.), *The New and the Multiple* (pp. 1–32). Chinese University Press.

Zola, E. (1901). *The Monomaniac*. Hutchinson & Company (Original work published 1901).

INDEX

Abrahamic religions 65
abstinence 59
Achaemenid Empire 47
Achaemenis 48
activation 79
aesthetic experience 25, 26, 96
aesthetics 26, 28, 30, 31, 34, 40, 73, 83, 84, 91
Afghanistan 7
afterlife 18–23, 25, 28, 34–39, 41, 52, 61, 62, 64, 65, 68, 71, 76, 83, 100
Alfonso VI of Castile 6
al-Mubāḥathāt ("The Discussions," Bahmanyar bin Marzban) 9
analytical approach 55
analytic geometry 54
"Answering the Question: What Is Enlightenment?" (Beantwortung der Frage: Was ist Aufklärung?, Kant)) 81
anti-aesthetic asceticism 27
Aquinas, Thomas 8
Arabic language 7
archaeological investigations 47
Arendt, Hannah 68, 69, 83, 84
aristocracy 6
Aristotelian 23

Aristotle 8, 80
art 15, 23, 24, 26, 31, 45, 49, 50, 54, 59, 61, 63, 72, 83–86, 96–98, 100, 101, 104, 106, 108
Art as Experience (Dewey) 15
asceticism 27, 28, 34, 53, 58, 109
Ash'arite synthesis 78
Asian countries 8
Attar 82
attention 29, 40, 72–76
Aurelius, Marcus 107
Aurobindo 79
authority 6, 16, 33, 37, 42, 70, 106
Avicenna (Ibn Sina) 7, 9, 10, 27, 51
awareness 70, 72, 75, 78, 80, 89

Bahmanyar bin Marzban 9, 27
Battle of Hastings (1086) 5
beauty 15, 24–28, 31, 34, 38, 43, 50, 68, 83, 84, 95–97, 101, 103
being and becoming 42
being and existence 1, 14, 25, 26, 31, 40, 42, 45, 51, 53, 55, 60, 73, 78, 83

INDEX

belief system 18, 28, 37, 81
Bell, Catherine 17
Bercovitch, Sacvan 93
Bergson, Henri 30, 44
big bang 45
Al Biruni 7
Bi Sheng 6
Bloch, Maurice 16
Bologna 6
Book of Optics (Ibn al-Haytham) 7
Byzantine empire 5

Camus, Albert 12
Canute (King) 5
Carnap, Rudolf 44
Carolingian Empire 6
Catholic Church 6
celestial bodies movement 24
China 5, 6
choices 21, 22, 24, 31, 36, 38, 46, 61, 76, 77, 80, 81, 102, 103
Christianity 8
Coming Victory of Democracy, The (Mann) 72
Concerning the Spiritual in Art (Kandinsky) 108
Confucian practice 6
Confucius 90
consciousness 21, 40, 49, 78, 80, 86, 102, 103
conventional thinking 60
cosmic bodies' movement 60
cosmos cycles 24, 62, 63
Council of Toulouges 6
courage 22, 23
creative space 3, 12, 14–50, 62, 63, 67, 73, 74, 83, 84, 88, 89, 91, 96, 100, 106
creativity 14–18, 20, 22, 24, 29, 30, 35, 43, 49, 52, 57, 65, 67, 70, 73, 74, 76, 79, 80, 85, 86, 88, 94, 96, 97, 101–104, 107

Crisis in Culture, The (Arendt) 84
critical thinking 89

Daryaee, Touraj 47
death 18–22, 25, 40, 63, 64, 67, 71, 101, 102, 107
democracy 72, 105
Descartes, René 54
destruction 18–20, 103
Dewey, John 15
discovery 12, 16, 64, 67
distraction 74, 76
dogmatic ideology 22, 28, 35, 52, 54, 55, 62, 83, 87, 89, 103, 106
dullness 75, 76
duration 30
dwelling 1–2

Eastern Orthodoxy 5
Ebrahim 9
Egypt 6, 7
Einstein, Albert 43, 44
El Cid 6
Emerson, R. W. 93
England 5
Enlightenment 81, 91, 102, 109
Eno, Brian 98
Epicurean agnosticism 60
eternal life 19, 37
Euclidian geometry 53
Europe 5, 8
evil 27, 31–33, 37, 67, 73, 74, 77, 86, 92, 93, 101

Al-Farabi 8, 10
fatalism 77, 92
Fatimid caliphate 7
Fisher, John 18
Fitzgerald, Edward 3
frame of reference 43–45
France, Kingdom of 6
Francis (Pope) 94

INDEX

Frankish Carolingian kings 6
freedom of thought 12, 42, 52
freethinking 1, 10, 12, 28, 54, 89, 91, 93, 94, 96, 100
free will 21, 24, 38, 59–61, 81, 92, 103

GDP 8
Germany 7
al-Ghazali, Abu Hamid 10, 28, 51–53
Ghaznavid campaigns 6
Ghaznavid dynasty 7
God 14, 31–34, 55, 59, 70, 92, 102
Godin Tepe 47
Graham, Thomas 101
Gregorian Calendar 11
Guernica (Picasso) 84
Guthrie, Stewart 39

hadith 32
Al-Hakim bi-Amr Allah 6
al-Ḥallāj, al-Ḥusayn ibn Manṣūr 59
happiness 16, 17, 20, 23, 27, 34, 37, 46, 52, 53, 60, 64, 69–73, 79–82, 86, 87, 89, 101, 102, 107
Harthacnut (King) 5
Hawking, Stephen 45
Hedayat, Sadeq 81
hedonism 50, 55, 64, 70, 75, 91, 101
Hegel 85
hegemony 12, 105, 106
Heian period 6, 7
Heidegger 1–2
Henry II (King) 7
Heraclitus 93
Herodotus 48
Hölderlin 2
human characteristics 39
humanistic approach 97

humanity 14, 67, 73, 78, 100, 105
(King) Husraw and Page 47, 48

Ibn al-Haytham 7
Ibn Arabī 78
Île-de-France 6
immutability 32, 61, 85
India 5–7
individual humanism 72
individualism 93
individuality 79, 93, 104
individuation 53, 68, 69, 76, 79, 93, 106
injustice 71
institutionalization 17, 94
Iran 42
Islam 11, 27, 32, 49
Islamic jurists 42, 58, 61, 63
Islamic mysticism 77, 100, 106, 108
Islamic orthodoxy 82, 89
Islamic society 59
Italy *see* Bologna

Jalali Calendar 11, 61
Japan 6
Jerusalem 7
joy 16, 24, 25, 28, 29, 34, 38, 46, 71, 86, 87, 94, 103, 107
Jung, Carl 93
al-Juwayni 10

Kandinsky, W. 108
Kant, Emmanuel 77, 78, 81, 91
Khayyam, Omar (Abu'l Fath. Omar ibn Ibrāhīm Khayyām): as astronomer 24; *On Being and Necessity* 9; birth and life 3–13; commitment to intellectual work 52, 53; creating harmony 3, 4, 23, 69, 95, 96; definition of life 70–71, 95; enthusiasm

for tranquility and peace 67–98, 104; influence of Zoroastrianism 27; love of wine 55–57; as mathematician 2–3, 54, 68; philosophical work 1, 18, 23, 26, 31–33, 38, 43, 61, 63; poetry 2, 3, 12, 14, 22–31, 34, 37, 42, 43, 46, 54, 56, 60, 61, 63, 70, 73, 76, 81, 84, 86, 91, 92, 97; protection from traditional Islamic jurists and persecution 42; against religious establishment 51–52, 58, 70; *Rubāʿiyyāt* 3, 18, 26, 37, 38, 63, 83, 85, 87, 88; scientific work 1–3, 23, 27, 38, 43, 54, 55, 61, 67, 81; stylometric analysis 110–115; worldview 15, 18, 23, 28, 44, 46, 49, 52, 53, 55, 68, 72, 76, 90, 93–96, 98, 100–103, 106; *see also individual entries*

Khosraw I (King) 48

Kimball, Charles 33

King, Martin Luther, Jr. 103

Kitāb al-taḥṣīll ("The Summation," Bahmanyar bin Marzban) 9

knowledge 1, 9, 12, 19, 23, 36, 42–45, 56, 61, 64, 67, 70, 71, 73, 79, 81–83, 88, 89, 91, 100, 102, 107

Lee, Bruce 57–58

liberation 12, 16, 40, 62, 68, 69, 71, 89, 90, 95, 102, 104, 107

life 15, 20, 24–26, 30, 31, 36–40, 42, 49, 52, 53, 62–64, 68, 71, 76–79, 81, 87, 91, 92; earthly 22, 23; meaningful 46

logic 10

Malik Shah 11

Mann, Thomas 71, 72

Masnavi (Rumi) 59

material culture 48

mathematics 53, 54

Mecca 11

Meditations (Aurelius) 107

Men in Dark Times (Arendt) 68

mental process 25

metaphysical world 58, 62

metaphysics 52

modern science 23

modern technology 71

moments 1, 18–20, 22, 24–26, 34, 36, 39–40, 45, 46, 52, 53, 56, 62, 70, 78, 83, 84, 87, 89, 101, 106

Monomaniac, The (Zola) 105

mortality 73

al-Mulk, Nizam 10

Muslim world 5, 7, 10, 12, 51

mystery 24–26, 38, 90

Nezamiye school 10, 11

Nezamiye's rule 11

Nietzsche, Friedrich 40, 41, 71, 75, 96

Nishabur 8–9, 11–12

non-Euclidean geometries 54

nonexistence 32, 33, 38–39

nonhuman events 39

Normans 5

nothingness 45–46

Now, problem of 44–45

nowness 45, 49, 61–63

obedience 16, 20, 33, 34, 64, 65, 70, 84, 100, 102, 103

occasionalism 10

Ommayad period 59

paper making techniques 10

passivity 20, 29, 40, 65, 77–79, 81, 88

Persia 7, 8, 47, 48

INDEX

Persian(s) 48; culture 47, 48, 59; history 47; identity 7
philosophy 8, 10, 14, 23, 26, 41, 42, 51, 54, 83, 100, 108
Picasso, Pablo 84, 85
Pliny 48
pluralism 12, 93
political parties 106
powerlessness 40
prejudice 43
procrastination 77
Puritan school of thought 58, 59
Pyrrhonism 88

Qāḍī Abū Naṣr 31
quantum theory 46
"Quest for Peace and Justice, The" (King) 103
Qur'ān 32, 77

Rajaraja Chola (King) 6
Rajendra Chola I (King) 6
rationalism 61, 71, 82
rationalist tradition 51
rationality 10, 23, 31, 38, 49, 55, 58, 59, 64, 67, 71, 74, 89, 97, 98, 100, 102
Razi 14
realism 67
reality 35, 36, 42, 49, 59, 65, 104
rebellion 16, 17, 20, 49, 50, 57, 64, 68, 83, 103
red wine 48
religion 33, 79, 82, 94; advocacy 28; doctrine 36; instrumentalization of 12; orthodoxy 26, 27–29, 41, 42, 61, 64, 77, 85, 87, 89, 93, 100, 105; practices 33, 102; studies 11
Remaining Signs of Past Centuries, The (Al Birouni) 13n1

ressentiment 40
restraints 53
Rex Teutonicorum 7
rhython 47
Rites of Assent, The (Bercovitch) 93
ritualization 17, 102
rituals 16–18, 29, 43, 62, 69, 72, 79, 89, 94, 104
Roman Catholicism 5
romanticism 23
Rosenfeld, B. A. 54
Rumi 59

salvation 37, 50, 52, 62, 72, 79, 95
Sasanian Empire 7, 47
Schopenhauer 71
science 10, 23, 44–45, 51, 59, 61, 72, 73, 83, 97, 100, 108
self-determinism 77
self-incurred immaturity 81
Seljuk dynasty 7, 10
Seneca, L. A. 74
Shahnameh (Ferdowsi) 7
Shahpur I (King) 8
Sharia orthodoxy 11, 12
Sheikhs 35, 36
Shiism 33
Sicily 8
Silk Road 8
skepticism 11, 34, 51, 58, 81, 82, 88, 89, 93
social change 17
social hierarchy 16, 47, 87
social space 17
social status quo 16
Song dynasty 6
sovereignty 73
Spain 6, 8
spirituality 100–101, 107–108
spiritual materialism 101
suffering 28, 29, 31, 35, 38, 59, 65, 67, 68, 70–72, 86, 92, 97, 102
Sufis 35, 36, 58, 82

INDEX

Sufism 26, 58, 59, 77, 82, 89
Sultan Sanjar 12
Summa Theologica (Aquinas) 8
superstitious beliefs 42, 43, 100, 106
Sweet, Alec Stone 17
Syria 7

Tale of Genji, The 7
Tang dynasty 6
terrestrial life 79
theory of relativity 43–45
Thus Spoke Zarathustra (Nietzsche and Kaufmann) 41
time 26, 29, 31, 33, 43–47, 52, 56, 61, 70, 74, 78, 87; theory of 30
Timpe, Kevin 21
transcendental power 100, 102, 104
transformative power 20
Truce of God 6
truth 26, 28, 32, 34
Two Essays on Analytical Psychology (Jung) 93

uniformity 37, 50, 68, 76, 94
universe 43, 45, 46, 60, 64, 82
University of Bologna 6

Viking age 5
violence 6, 29, 31, 33, 67–69, 80, 83, 86, 87, 94, 97, 98, 103, 104, 106

Wallace, Davis Foster 75
Webber, Max 68
Western world 5
Westminster Abbey 5
Westminster Shorter Catechism 32
white wine 48
wine 46; drinking 47, 55–57; making 47
wisdom 60, 67, 92
world economy 8
World Health Organization 80
worldliness 59

Youschkevitch, A. P. 54
Yukio Mishima 101

Zeitgeist 83, 85–87
Zhenzong (King) 6
Zizhi Tongjian 6
Zola, E. 105
Zolian machine-monster 105–106
Zoroastrianism 27

For Product Safety Concerns and Information please contact our EU representative GPSR@taylorandfrancis.com
Taylor & Francis Verlag GmbH, Kaufingerstraße 24, 80331 München, Germany

www.ingramcontent.com/pod-product-compliance
Lightning Source LLC
Chambersburg PA
CBHW061719300426
44115CB00014B/2748